DARK FLORIDA

Animal Attacks, Historic Murders, Deadly Disasters and Other Calamities

ALAN BROWN

THE
History
PRESS

Published by The History Press
Charleston, SC
www.historypress.com

First published 2023

Manufactured in the United States

ISBN 9781467154574

Library of Congress Control Number: 2023934790

This book is dedicated to my three grandsons: Cade, Owen and Samuel.

CONTENTS

INTRODUCTION

F lorida has a number of features that set it apart from the rest of the United States. Florida has the longest coastline in the continental United States. Not only is Florida the flattest state in the Union, but it also has the lowest highest point. Everglades National Park is the largest tropical wilderness in the entire county. The only living coral barrier reef in the continental United States is the Florida Reef. More deposits of potash have been discovered in Florida than in any other U.S. state. The state's tropical climate, sunny beaches, five-star restaurants and nationally known theme parks have made Florida one of the country's favorite tourist destinations, second only to California.

However, Florida also has a dark side that is known primarily by the residents of Florida. Florida has over half of the total shark attacks in the entire United States. Florida also ranks third in the total number of animal attacks in the United States. Prohibition-era gangsters, like the Ashley Gang, Al Capone and the Barker-Karpis Gang, lived and died in Florida. Predatory human beings have spent time in Florida as well, including serial killers Ted Bundy and Aileen Wuornos. Tuberculosis and yellow fever epidemics have claimed thousands of lives here. More hurricanes have made landfall in Florida than in any other state since the creation of the Saffir-Simpson scale in 1851. Dozens of ships and airplanes have vanished in the area bounded by Miami, Bermuda and Puerto Rico known as the Bermuda Triangle. The hanging tree growing through the roof of Captain Tony's Saloon and the Castillo de San Marcos attract thousands of visitors each year. Finally, Florida has some of the most legendary cemeteries in the country, like the Huguenot Cemetery in St. Augustine and Spring Hill Cemetery in Brooksville.

For some people, Florida is the place where writers like Ernest Hemingway, Marjorie Kinnan Rawlings and Zora Neale Hurston lived. For others, it is the home of Mickey Mouse and former president Harry S. Truman. However, if you are one of these people who enjoy probing the more sinister sides of vacation getaways, pour a glass of orange juice, pull up a lawn chair and enjoy *Dark Florida: Death and Destruction in the Sunshine State.*

1

ANIMAL ATTACKS

ALLIGATOR ATTACKS

By the 1950s, the American alligator had been almost hunted to extinction for hides in the Southeast. In 1967, it was listed as endangered throughout its range under the Endangered Species Preservation Act. Today, approximately 1.5 alligators inhabit Florida's lakes, rivers, canals and swamps. Thousands of them live in and around the Everglades. According to Ricky L. Langley of the North Carolina Department of Health and Human Services, alligators are, as a rule, not aggressive toward human beings: "Smaller alligators usually bite only once; however, up to one-third of all attacks may involve repeated bites." Alligators tend to lose their fear of people when food is involved. The first recorded fatal alligator attack in the United States took place near Sarasota. The number of alligator bites has risen from six per year between 1971 and 1986 to ten per year from 1987 through 2017. According to the Ecological Society of America, human population size was a reliable predictor of alligator attack rates during the period between 1988 and 2016. The increased development of areas used by alligators is definitely a factor in the increased number of attacks.

A number of high-profile alligator attacks have occurred in the twenty-first century. In 2012, a ten-foot-long alligator grabbed the arm of Kaleb Langdale, seventeen, while he was swimming in the Caloosahatchee River west of Lake Okeechobee. The alligator bit off the boy's arm in the struggle.

Reports of alligator attacks are on the rise on Florida because of the increased development of the creatures' habitat. *Wikimedia Commons.*

Wildlife officers killed the alligator and removed the arm from its stomach, but doctors were unable to reattach it.

The rising number of alligator attacks really came to the public's attention on June 14, 2016, when two-year-old Lane Graves was building sandcastles on the beach at Walt Disney World's Grand Florida Resort and Spa. Lane had just bent over to scoop sand out of a bucket when a large alligator burst from the surface of the water and dragged the little boy into the Seven Seas Lagoon. Dozens of guests, including Lane's horrified parents, witnessed the incident. When Lane's body was retrieved seventeen hours later, the medical examiner concluded that he had died of a traumatic neck injury and drowning. Immediately, signs were posted around the lagoon warning visitors of the danger of alligators. In addition, a wall was built around the lagoon. It turned out, though, that 6 alligators had been removed from the lagoon a few days before. Over the next five years, wildlife trappers removed 226 "nuisance alligators" from Disney World's property.

Another bloodcurdling attack took place in 2021 when a forty-seven-year-old transient named Sean Thomas McGuiness swam into a lake near a disc golf course late at night at John S. Taylor Park. He had been making a living selling Frisbees to people who played at the disc golf course. On this particular night, McGuiness was killed by one of the alligators that frequented the lake. The next morning, a man walking his dog by the lake discovered McGuinness's mutilated remains.

That same year, an eighty-seven-year-old woman, Rose Marie Wiegand, was walking her dog near her house in Englewood, Florida. All of a sudden, she slipped and fell into a pond by the Boca Royale Golf and Country Club shortly before 8:00 p.m. Within just a few moments, two alligators lunged at the woman and killed her. Later, the alligators were removed from the pond by the Florida Fish and Wildlife Conservation Commission.

One of Florida's alligators has become the stuff of legend. Two-Toed Tom is the state's most infamous alligator. The reptile received that moniker after losing all but two toes in a steel trap. The first story about Two-Toed Tom surfaced in 1922. According to Carl Carmer's book *Stars Fell on Alabama*, Two-Toed Tom was a red-eyed fourteen-foot alligator that preyed on livestock and farmers in Alabama. Legend has it that the alligator raped and consumed women as well. Several failed attempts were made to kill or capture the creature. For example, an ex-military sniper spent a week hiding in a blind in an attempt to catch the monster gator off-guard. Carmer also

In 2021, eighty-seven-year-old Rose Wiegand was attacked by two alligators from a pond at the Royale Golf and Country Club. *Wikimedia Commons.*

relates the tale of a farmer, Pap Haines, who tossed buckets of dynamite into the pond where the reptile was living.

The increased hunting pressure is believed to have forced Two-Toed Tom to flee Alabama and take up residence in Hammock Lake between Esto, Florida, and Monroe, Florida. Two-Toed Tom made himself a nuisance by attacking and eating livestock. He was also believed to bellow at the Alabama-Florida Lumber Company mill's whistle as well. According to E.W. "Judge" Carswell's book *Homesteading*, a couple of boys fired their .22-caliber rifles at the beast with no effect. In fact, many hunters swore that their bullets simply bounced off the gator's hide. Two-Toed Tom's last appearance was in an article published in the News Journal in 1973. Supposedly, the alligator was sighted near Red Head, Florida. Carswell believes that Two-Toed Tom might actually be a composite of all of the alligators people have encountered in the little Panhandle town.

Like many small towns, Esto has capitalized on its signature legend. Since 1987, a festival has been held in Florida celebrating the exploits of Two-Toed Tom. Each year, the festival offers locals and out-of-towners an opportunity to enjoy entertainment, food and storytellers who regale their listeners with tales about their legendary swamp monster.

THE FLORIDA PANTHER

The Florida panther, a subspecies of the cougar, became Florida's state animal in 1981. Florida panthers can be found in a 200-mile expanse of pinewoods, hammocks and swamp forests in Southwest Florida. The home range of most panthers is roughly 275 miles. They can run thirty-five miles per hour in short bursts. Adult panthers can reach an average weight of 150 pounds and a length of seven feet. Although they prefer deer and wild hogs, panthers have been known to eat armadillos, raccoons, snakes and even alligators. As the panther's habitat has shrunk, attacks on domesticated animals have become common. The Florida Fish and Wildlife Conservation Commission reported forty-nine panther attacks on pets and "hobby livestock" like goats, donkeys and miniature horses in 2017. For example, Golden Gate Estates, a suburb of Naples, lies in proximity to Everglades National Wildlife Refuge. In 2021, a panther jumped over a four-foot chain-link fence and snatched a pet goat named Daisy out of a backyard. The panther had to leave the goat behind when one of its

The number of attacks on domesticated animals by Florida panthers is increasing as civilization continues encroaching on their territory. *Wikimedia Commons.*

hooves became caught in the fence, but Daisy died of her injuries a short while later. In 2018, a panther killed a 500-pound pony named Maximus in Gold Gate Estates. A pet dog lost one of its eyes in a panther attack in Golden Gates Estates in 2021.

There has never been a documented panther attack on a human being in Florida. However, in 2014, the former chairman of the Board for the Florida Sportsmen, Byron Maharrey, claimed that he was sitting in a chair, waiting for his decoys to lure in a big gobbler, when he was knocked forward out of his chair. As the animal ran off, Maharrey caught a glimpse of a long tail and tawny fur. He believed that the three layers of clothing he was wearing at the time prevented him from suffering more than a four-inch wound on his left shoulder and two punctures on his left thigh.

Attacks in places like Golden Gate Estates indicate that the Florida panther is making a comeback. In 1991, the panther population was estimated around 20 animals. By 2021, the panther population in Florida had grown considerably, with estimates ranging from 120 to 220. Their greatest threat to living in proximity to human beings is cars. To protect the Florida panther, legislators passed the Florida Wildlife Corridor Act on July 1, 2021, which provided $300 million for land acquisition.

SHARK ATTACKS

In 2021, almost 40 percent of all shark attacks occurred in Florida. The twenty-eight cases reported in the International Shark Attack File made up 60 percent of the attacks in the United States that year. Most of these victims were attacked by blacktips and bull sharks, which prefer shallow waters. Blacktips, which are less aggressive, average three to five feet in length. They migrate from North Carolina to South Florida. The large number of shark attacks in Florida in 2021 may be due in part to the fact that many people, eager to escape the COVID-19 pandemic restrictions, returned to the public beaches, which were closed in 2020.

Robert Hueter, chief scientist at Shark Data Organization, believes that other factors might also account for the high numbers of shark attacks in Florida. Because of the increase in conservation efforts, the fish that sharks feed on are making a comeback. Hueter said, "When those schools make their way in towards the beach, sharks come with them." He also believes that many people have become less wary of sharks because of depleted shark populations. "The sharks have always been there, to some extent, but their numbers have been much lower than they are right now because of overfishing over the last 30–40 years," Hueter said. In recent years, the size of the shark population has increased due to fisheries' concerted management efforts. Another reason why more people are exposing themselves to shark attacks is connected to global warming. As temperatures rise, more people flock to the beaches. The proximity of the Gulf Stream to the shore could also be a factor in the high number of shark attacks. In 2021, surfers and board sports enthusiasts were most likely to become the victims of shark attacks, followed by swimmers, body surfers and snorkelers/free divers. Some experts believe that sharks are attracted to large exposed areas of skin. According to the Florida Museum of Natural History, most shark attacks are cases of mistaken identity. Experts have arrived at this conclusion because in most cases, sharks tend

Blacktip sharks, like the one pictured here, and bull sharks are responsible for many of the attacks on human beings. *Wikimedia Commons.*

to bite once and then swim off. These bites are called "test bites." Attacks also occur when sharks are attempting to defend themselves, especially when a human being gets in their way. Juvenile sharks tend to bite more impulsively because they are smaller and, therefore, more likely to be preyed on by larger creatures. Swimming between dusk and dawn is the best way, experts say, to avoid shark attacks.

According to the International Shark Attack File, between 1845 and 2016, Florida had more than eight hundred recorded shark attacks, thirty-six of which were fatal. The first recorded shark attack in Florida's history was reported in the September 10, 1845 edition of the *Tioga Eagle*. A shark killed a man known only as Nickerson while he was fishing with nets. The first attack on multiple people was reported on August 16, 1849. A man named Mansfield swam over to two women who were being attacked by a shark. He saved one of them but died while trying to save the second. In 1853, a captain from Charleston, South Carolina, was near Fernando Bay in Nassau County when he was knocked overboard and eaten by a shark that was following the ship.

Between 1901 and 1930, only 29 percent of reported shark attacks were fatal. Belton Larkin was fishing for tarpons from his boat when he fell overboard and was nearly cut in two by sharks. In 1917, the *Washington Post* reported that William Sinker was devoured before a huge crowd of spectators. Sinker was the first victim of a shark attack in Key West. On June 20, 1934, eight-year-old Richard Clark Best Jr. was standing in chest-deep water when bystanders heard screaming. He died of shark bites in his hips. In 1952, a twenty-six-year-old lieutenant in the U.S. Army in Fort Rucker, Alabama, named James Neal was spearfishing off the coast of Panama City with five other divers. After a few minutes, the other divers noticed that Neal was no longer with them. The next day, searchers located Neal's equipment, but his body never turned up. Sharks certainly may have been involved in Neal's disappearance. No deadly shark attacks were reported from 1962 until 1976. In 1976, two brothers from Tennessee, Ricky and Michael Karras, vanished while swimming near the Jacksonville Fishing Club. Only Michael's body washed ashore. He had been bitten in the shoulder and the leg. He is thought to have been killed by either a bull shark or a hammerhead shark. In 1981, four people were sailing on a catamaran off the Ormond Beach coast when suddenly, the craft began taking in water. With no life jackets, they had to hang on to the edge of the craft the entire night. The next day, the group decided to make an attempt to swim to shore. Christy Wapniarski, the weakest swimmer, ran out of energy and began splashing and kicking in the water. All at once, she began screaming, "Shark!" At the same moment, the water around her turned crimson. Her boyfriend reported later that a shark had ripped off her leg. He and another member of the group tried to swim her back to shore but were forced to leave her behind when they became exhausted. Her body was never found.

In 2005, Jaimie Daigle, fourteen, was swimming 200 to 250 feet offshore in Miramar Beach when a shark feeding on a school of fish lunged at her. A fifty-four-year-old surfer named Tim Dicus became alarmed when the spot where the girl had been swimming turned bright red. By the time he got to her, she was floating facedown. He placed her on his board and swam her over to a raft, which took her ashore. Daigle was later pronounced dead at the hospital.

The number of shark attacks in Florida in the twenty-first century has shown no signs of diminishing. In 2010, a lifeguard in Stuart, Florida, decided to investigate when he saw a man lying on the sail of a kite board about a quarter mile offshore. Several sharks circled around the lifeguard as he tried to swim the injured man, Stephen Schaefer, to shore. Schaeffer was later pronounced dead from puncture wounds to the femoral artery. In 2015, the Florida Fish and Wildlife Commission reported that a great white shark swam under a twenty-two-foot-long boat eight and a half miles from the shore and pushed it several feet. Neither the owner of the boat, Scott Fitzgerald, nor the shark was injured. On March 9, 2022, a five- or six-foot-long blacktip shark bit a twenty-one-year-old man while he was fishing in waist-deep water. He was bitten on his left knee and calf. On June 30, 2022, Addison Bethea, a seventeen-year-old girl, was scalloping with her family in Keaton Beach when she was attacked by a shark. At the time, she was standing in water five feet deep. The wounds to her leg were so severe that it had to be amputated just above the right knee. On July 2022, a twenty-eight-year-old man was surfing in New Smyrna Beach at 11:43 a.m. when he fell off his board and was bitten by a shark. Doctors determined that his bite was minor. In July 2022, Tasa Summers, forty, and her boyfriend were waking in the water along the shore in Daytona Beach when suddenly, she felt pain in her leg. She realized immediately that she had been bitten by a shark. To keep the shark from biting her again, her boyfriend fended it off while

In 2015, a great white shark swam under a twenty-two-foot-long boat and pushed it several feet. *Wikimedia Commons.*

she returned to shore. She ended up with eight stitches in her leg. On July 25, 2022, thirty-three-year-old Bryan Olivares was bitten in his foot while walking off the coast of Daytona Beach. Later, doctors found that a shark had damaged a nerve and sliced his tendon. Two days later, thirteen-year-old Fischer Hrico was lobster fishing with his family when a shark bit him in his face. He had to have ten stiches in his lip. In early August 2022, ten-year-old Jameson Reeder Jr. and his family were snorkeling in the Florida Keys when an eight-foot bull shark bit him in his knee. While the boy was lying on a swimming noodle, his family tied a tourniquet on his leg to slow the bleeding. His leg had to be amputated below the knee.

On June 29, 2022, Lindsay Bruns, thirty-five, was in a boat on a family vacation in Sawyer Key. Later that afternoon, she jumped off the boat into the ocean for a swim with her husband, Luke. Seconds after she hit the water, her husband was shocked to see a cloud of blood billowing around her. As soon as he got her back in the boat, he could tell that her leg had severe lacerations. During the twenty-minute boat ride back to shore, he applied pressure to her wound. Bruns was given a blood transfusion on the way to the hospital. Fortunately, she made a full recovery.

INVASIVE SNAKE SPECIES

Snakes have always been part of Florida's ecosystem. Some of them, like the eastern coral snake, the harlequin coral snake, the eastern copperhead, the Florida cottonmouth, the pygmy rattlesnake, the timber rattlesnake and the eastern diamondback rattlesnake, are venous. According to *The Florida Handbook*, roughly three hundred venomous snakebites occur annually in Florida. Approximately 90 percent of these snakebites occur during the summer. The average age of snakebite victims is twenty to twenty-five. More than 1,300 children suffer snakebites each year on the average, with one out of four attacks occurring in Florida and Texas. Generally, rattlesnakes are the most venomous snakes and the most likely to cause death.

While these snakes are capable of inflicting severe pain and even death on people and pets, they play an important role in the state's ecosystems. Unlike Florida's native snakes, invasive species of nonindigenous snakes tend to be destructive to native animals and their food sources. Five species of invasive snakes have made Florida their home. Two of them—Javan file snakes and Brahminy blindsnakes—are small and have done little harm to the environment. Boa constrictors are more destructive because of their size. Introduced into Florida through the pet trade in the 1960s and '70s, boa constrictors grow between seven and thirteen feet long. They feed on birds, rodents and many other mammals. African rock pythons were introduced into Florida via the pet trade in 2002. African rock pythons are one of the largest species of snakes in the world, reaching up to a length of six meters (ten to sixteen feet). Because of their immense size, African rock pythons eat anything they can catch. By far the most invasive snake in Florida is the Burmese python, which is found primarily in and around the Everglades ecosystem in South Florida, mostly because of the subtropical climate and the absence of predators. Burmese pythons were first introduced to Florida through the pet trade in 1979, when many of these snakes were imported to Miami from Southeast Asia. Once the pythons became too large to be manageable, their owners released them into the wild, where they easily adapted to their new surroundings. Their invasive presence was really noticed until the 1990s.

In 2021, the exotic animal trade was banned in Florida, but by this time, the Burmese pythons had already established a foothold in the state. Estimated numbers of the python population in Florida run from ten

Burmese pythons were introduced into the Florida Everglades through the pet trade in 1979. *Wikimedia Commons.*

thousand to hundreds of thousands. The python population is difficult to assess because their camouflage coloring helps them blend in with their environment and because they tend to favor relatively inaccessible places to live, like the Florida wetlands. Consisting of cypress swamps, small limestone islands, sawgrass prairies and mangrove forest, the Everglades stretch more than one hundred miles north to south. Because Burmese pythons are the largest snakes, growing up to twenty feet long and weighing as much as two hundred pounds, they eat whatever they can catch and fit into their mouths. They kill small animals by biting them near the head and swallowing them whole; they kill large animals by crushing them in their coils before ingesting them. Wildlife biologists estimate that the Burmese pythons' voracious appetite is responsible for the 90 to 99 percent drop in the population of small opossums, raccoons and bobcats in 1997.

The South Florida Management District has found that the most workable solution to Burmese python problem is python hunters. To date, the SFWMD has one hundred paid contractors, who earn between $10 and $15 an hour as an incentive for each python they catch. So far, the Burmese python hunter program has taken approximately ten thousand snakes.

2

EPIDEMICS

YELLOW FEVER (1887–88)

Key West, Tampa and Jacksonville

Yellow fever is a disease that is brought on by a virus in the family Flaviviridae. It is spread to people through the bite of the *Aedes aegypti* mosquito. The disease was introduced to the United States through water barrels brought to this country on ships from countries with endemic yellow fever. Symptoms include nausea, muscle pain, vomiting and headaches. A small percentage of people develop the life-threatening form of the disease, which includes internal bleeding, high fevers, kidney damage and jaundice, or a "yellowing" of the skin. Jaundice is produced through liver damage. The disease is not spread through casual contact, although people can contract yellow fever through infected needles.

Florida was ravaged by yellow fever epidemics in 1887–88. At this time, physicians did not know that the disease was transmitted to people by mosquitos. In May 1887, a yellow fever epidemic reached Key West after passing through Havana. Tampa reacted to the news with overwhelming fear. City officials prohibited the transportation of freight, baggage, the U.S. mail and people to Tampa from Key West and Havana. On June 9, the city set up quarantine camps where people traveling by boat from Key West and Havana to Tampa were detained for fifteen days. As Key West's epidemic began to

subside in mid-August, public officials
began to breathe a sigh of relief, despite the
fact that Dr. John P. Wall, a local physician,
had reported the case of a Black attendant
at Egmont station who had taken sick, Dr.
Wall believed that illegal trade had brought
on the disease, not legitimate trade, like
Henry Plant's shipping line.

In September 1887, Charlie Turk from
Ybor City became the first person to die
of "yellow jack" in Tampa. Turk was a
barber and fruit smuggler. Later on, Turk
would be blamed for the city's epidemic.
The first case of yellow fever in Tampa was
an Italian fruit dealer named Louis Moses.
Four other fruit dealers became infected
later on. At the time, Dr. Wall was out of
town. When he returned on September
25, Tampa was buzzing with rumors of an
incipient epidemic. By September 29, Wall

This cartoon drawn by Jack
Morgan depicts the devastating
effects of the yellow fever epidemic
of 1887–88 in Key West, Tampa
and Jacksonville. *PICRYL.*

had reported five cases of the disease; by October 4, Wall had seen seven cases.
Even though Wall played down the rumors of an epidemic, he did advise
people who were not immune to yellow fever to flee the city on October 5.
On October 6, the *Tampa Journal* conceded that rampant fear had taken over.
Yet the editor of the *Tampa Journal* played down the severity of the epidemic.
On October 8, the story of Tampa's epidemic appeared on the front page of
the *New York Times*. Newspapers throughout Florida condemned Dr. Wall and
the county board of health for creating a virtual stampede of citizens fleeing
Tampa. Dr. Wall was also criticized for proclaiming the presence of the disease
in Tampa. In the midst of the controversy, the cigar factories in Tampa stayed
open, and tobacco was removed from the list of quarantined items.

Still, the epidemic took its toll on the lives of the people of Tampa. By
October 24, eighty people had contracted the disease and forty-eight people
had died. A relief committee was organized to furnish wood and bread to
indigent people and to pay the hospital bills for needy patients. The relief
committee also provided jobs to unemployed people to keep the city streets clean.

When a light frost occurred in Tampa, many citizens and city officials
began to relax, thinking that the end of the epidemic was near. The city
council prohibited the return of refugees to Tampa until the county board

of health was assured that the city was safe. In January 1888, the *Tampa Journal* reported only three or four cases of yellow fever in Tampa. The relief committee reported its last fatality on January 11, 1888. Dr. Wall declared that the epidemic was over. However, the city's complacency was short-lived. On July 21, 1888, a commercial traveler, Adin E. Waterman, died of yellow fever in Tampa on July 21, 1888. His corpse was wrapped in a sheet coated with mercuric chloride and interred in a metal coffin. However, on July 28, 1888, a saloonkeeper, Richard D. McCormick, boarded a train from Tampa to Jacksonville. At the time, he was very sick. After he checked into a hotel, the president of the local board of health received word of McCormick's illness and had him sent to the "pest house" at Sands Hills. Dr. Wall insisted that McCormick had become infected in Plant City, not Tampa.

Nevertheless, McCormick was held responsible by many people for spreading yellow fever to Jacksonville in 1888. On August 8, four more cases of yellow fever were reported. Five more cases were reported on August 9 and three more cases on August 10. On that date, the Jacksonville Sanitary Association was created to act as a coordinating body with the other agencies. On August 12, the Jacksonville Sanitary Association commenced the work of "cleaning up" the city. Mounds of pine and tar were set afire to "purify the air." Working on the belief that concussion would destroy the germs, Wilson's battery of militia fired fifty rounds of ammunition. Workers sprayed streets with bichloride of mercury and coated hydrants, tree trunks, posts and curbs with a coating of disinfectant and lime. The association also organized a committee on sanitary policy and a committee to deal with claims of property damage.

Over the next few weeks, the disease intensified, finally reaching its peak in the week of September 19–25. During these seven days, 944 new cases and 70 deaths were reported. On September 5, the association issued a public plea for financial aid. Within a few weeks, the association received donations from forty-two states and from Ontario (Canada), London (England), and Darmstadt (Germany). With these funds, the association was able to form a committee on nurses, which enrolled 837 nurses. Surgeon-general J.B. Hamilton added sixteen physicians from other cities to the Medical Bureau, in addition to the eleven resident physicians.

Jacksonville also had to deal with the thousands of residents who would not or could not leave the city. Camps of refuge were established to induce people to leave the city, but they were not very popular. The federal government authorized the construction of two hundred houses at one of these camps—Camp Mitchell—seven miles outside of the city. However, construction was not completed until October, which meant that only 410 people occupied the houses. By the time the camp closed on December 15, only one death and a few cases of the disease were reported.

Another problem the association addressed was unemployment, which grew because business in Jacksonville had stagnated. The association created the Public Improvement Works, which employed a large number of Black people. One of the projects that the Public Improvement Works took on was the grading, widening and shelling of the Evergreen Cemetery Road. Some 1,600 men were hired to make improvements in Devall Street.

A particularly challenging problem was the destruction and disinfection of bedding, clothing and property. Workers burned mattresses, pillows and quilts. They also baked or boiled carpets and other bedding, The cost of these sanitary measures was covered by the U.S. government,

By October 1888, the number of new cases and deaths from yellow fever had appreciably declined. On October 31, the Sand Hills hospital was closed. To prevent refugees from returning to Jacksonville before the danger had passed, the contingent of 100 guards was increased to 433 guards in early October. Before the end of the month, these guards were supplemented with a cordon of mounted guards placed around Jacksonville.

New cases of yellow fever continued to decrease in early November, but as temperatures continued to rise later in the month, so did the number of cases. By the end of the month, city officials reported 112 new cases and 29 deaths. To make sure that the disease did not make a significant comeback in Jacksonville, the city hired 150 men and rented sixty wagons to commence with the fumigation of Jacksonville. After the refugees were allowed to return on December 15, the *Times-Union* and the *Savannah Morning News* reported that Jacksonville's yellow fever epidemic had resulted in 4,656 cases and 427 deaths.

THE GREAT WHITE PLAGUE (1917–45)

Key West

Tuberculosis is a contagious respiratory disease that mainly affects the lungs. The bacteria that cause the disease are spread through the air through coughing. People infected with latent TB cannot spread the disease to other people because the bacteria are inactive and, therefore, produce no symptoms. Active TB, which produces a variety of symptoms, can be spread to others. Most tuberculosis patients became infected with the disease from people with whom they came into contact. The symptoms, which can manifest weeks after infection with the TB bacteria, include the following: prolonged coughing, coughing up mucus or blood, chest pain, weight loss, chills, night sweats, fever and loss of appetite. Until the development of drugs such as para-aminosalicylic acid (PAS) and streptomycin, tuberculosis was a major health problem throughout the world.

Statistics for new cases and death rates from tuberculosis were first made public in 1917, when it was credited as being the primary cause of death in the state. Ironically, Florida is not only the state with a climate perfectly suited to the treatment of the disease but also one of the states with high numbers of deaths from tuberculosis. By 1923, tuberculosis was the second leading cause of death in the state. In the years that followed, the number of cases began to decline. In 1928, tuberculosis was the third major cause of death. By 1930, tuberculosis was the fifth leading cause of death in Florida. Although tuberculosis was no longer one of the top ten causes of death in Florida in the 1930s and the 1940s, it continued to claim large numbers of victims in the state. In 1935, the disease claimed more lives by half than

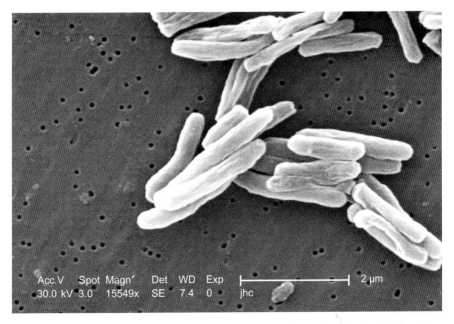

The bacteria responsible for the outbreak of tuberculosis in Key West between 1917 and 1945 is spread through the air by coughing. *Wikimedia Commons.*

automobile accidents, twice as many lives as malaria and twenty times more lives than typhoid. To combat the disease, the State Board of Health began making efforts to control the disease through mobile X-ray units. Educational materials, such as bulletins, posters, books and films, were made available to the public as well.

Although the State of Florida began making progress in its war against tuberculosis in the late 1930s and early 1940s, the disease was still a serious health problem in Key West. Even though clinics were opened in the city in the 1930s and access to health services was improved, the numbers of new cases of tuberculosis and the number of deaths from the disease continued to climb. Local physicians cited several different factors that impeded efforts to eradicate the disease. One of these problems was the lack of adequate hospital care in Key West. For most of the citizens of Key West, the only available hospital care, cottage hospitals, had closed. People sought medical care at the Marine Hospital instead, but after it closed in 1943, they were forced to go to civilian facilities that had not received approval by any medical organizations. To make matters worse, between 1940 and 1942, only four physicians were on staff at Key West. In 1942, the number of physicians in Key West increased to six, but four of them were elderly and one was uncertified. Only one received patients in his office. Recruiting better qualified doctors to Key West was difficult because the six physicians drove off anyone new who wanted to practice medicine there. Good nurses were in short supply in Key West as well. In her article "The Great White Plague: Tuberculosis in Key West, 1917–1945," author Maria Melssen says that no trained nurses were working in Key West in 1942

Melssen also cites the lifestyles of the populace as a contributing factor to Key West's health problems. For years, most of the people living in Key West were nomadic: tourists, bohemian types and military personal. Melssen writes, "Communities with a fluctuating population are at greater risk for illness, and such diverse, migratory populations have historically been perceived as threats to public health." Throughout the world, tuberculosis has thrived among populations such as these. Key West physician Dr. Pearse believed that the excessive drinking and violent behavior of many of the residents of Key West put them in "a state of medical jeopardy."

By the late 1940s, the death rate from tuberculosis in Key West had begun to decline. The development of "wonder drugs" like PAS and streptomycin was certainly a factor. However, the strengthening of the economy at this time was also responsible for the defeat of the disease. Construction projects initiated by the U.S. Navy brought new jobs to the city. The increasing numbers of tourists to the city and Key West's growing shrimping industry attracted more permanent residents to Key West and started a housing boom. Key West now had the financial means to improve its health care systems. Also, because fresh water was being piped in from the mainland, the citizens of Key West no longer had to depend on unsanitary cisterns.

By the twenty-first century, the presence of tuberculosis in Florida had greatly diminished. In 1992, Florida ranked fourth in the nation with 1,707 reported cases of tuberculosis. In 2009, 821 cases of tuberculosis were reported in Florida. Only 7 of these cases were from Key West. However, according to an article posted on businessinsider.com on July 9, 2012, the CDC reported that thirteen patients, six of whom were children, died from tuberculosis in a Jacksonville Hospital. The article went on to say that the Florida legislature cut the state health department's budget and closed A.G. Holley State Hospital, which had been treating tuberculosis patients for over fifty years. Articles such as this suggest that tuberculosis may not be as much of a threat as it was years ago, but ignoring it altogether brings consequences.

Spanish Flu (1918–19)

The Entire State of Florida

Caused by an H1N1 virus with genes of avian origin, the 1918 influenza epidemic went global between 1918 and 1919. The disease first made an appearance in the United States in members of the armed forces. Approximately one-third of the world's population—50 million people—contracted the virus. Around 675,000 Americans were infected with the disease. Because no vaccine was developed during the epidemic, non-pharmaceutical methods were used to control the disease, including quarantine, isolation, the use of disinfectants, personal hygiene and exposure to only small groups of people.

Florida made strides in the areas of industrialization and immigration in the two decades following the yellow fever epidemic of 1888. However, much of this progress was canceled out in 1918 when Florida, like the rest of world, began to feel the impact of the 1918 flu epidemic. Many health officials proclaimed throughout the world that the flu epidemic would peak around July. However, they soon realized that a second wave of the disease was on the horizon.

Mask-wearing was one of the precautions taken in Florida during the 1918–19 Spanish flu epidemic. *Library of Congress.*

In Florida, one-third of the population of Jacksonville contracted the flu. As a result, "No Spitting!" signs were posted all over the city by November 11, 1918—Armistice Day. Businesses where large numbers of people congregate, like vaudeville theaters, movie palaces, pool halls and saloons, were closed. Conversely, business was so good for coffin makers that they soon ran out of the materials used to make coffins. A Pensacola newspaper that once hailed Pensacola as "One of the Healthiest Cities on Map" in July 1918 lamented in October 1918 that "almost no spot was spared!" One-third of the students at the University of Florida in Gainesville came down with the disease, including the president, Albert Murphree. Catastrophes on a large scale, like plagues, were nothing new to the residents of St. Augustine. However, in 1918, the *St. Augustine Record of the Day* informed its readers that for the first time in the city's history, "churches, schools and theaters have been closed and public meetings canceled."

Parts of Florida that were normally considered to be insulated from large outbreaks of disease were also affected by the 1918 flu epidemic. Small towns had to face the sobering fact that the virus did not prey only on large urban centers. Twenty people died of the flue in Quincy, eight died in Kissimmee and four residents of Greenville died in one week. Floridians soon learned that the disease took both the weak and the powerful, such as Herbert Moore, the youngest member of the state legislature. The Seminoles were spared the wrath of the virus because of their isolation. However, after an airplane crashed in the Big Cypress in 1918, rescuers who arrived at the Seminole villages brought the virus with them, causing the death of ten Native Americans.

By the end of the epidemic in 1919, approximately 20,000 citizens of Tampa had contracted the flu; 283 Tampa residents died of the flu. Poor people who lived in close proximity to one another in Tampa were particularly vulnerable, like the workers in factories in West Tampa. African Americans were denied access to health care in hospitals in Tampa and many parts of Florida until near the end of the epidemic. In Tampa, a Black nurse named Clara Frye cared for flu victims in her own house. D.A. Dorsey, Tampa's first Black millionaire, converted his hotel in Overton into a field hospital for victims of the flu. The *Tampa Tribune* paid homage to the physicians who selflessly risked their lives to treat the city's sick and dying: "For devotion to duty, who except mothers and soldiers excels the family doctor…the Tampa doctors are the salt of the earth." It goes without saying that physicians in any health crisis would not be nearly as effective were it not for the nurses who assist them and put their own lives in peril as well.

COVID-19 PANDEMIC (2020–22)

The Entire State of Florida

According to the World Health Organization (WHO), the first outbreak of COVID-19 appeared in Wuhan, China, in 2019. The disease was caused by the SARS-CoV-2 virus. The disease first surfaced in the city of Wuhan in December 2019. It then spread throughout Asia and the rest of the world. The WHO declared the outbreak of a pandemic on March 11, 2020. COVID-19 is spread in the form of liquid particles coughed, breathed or sneezed into the air by infected persons. Symptoms of this respiratory disease include coughing, chills, muscle or body aches, fever, shortness of breath, fatigue, headaches, sore throat, congestion, loss of taste or

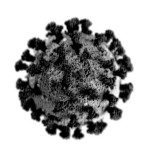

The first cases of COVID-19 in Florida were reported in Manatee and Hillsborough. *Wikimedia Commons.*

smell, nausea or vomiting, diarrhea and coughing up of phlegm. During the pandemic, residents of Florida and the rest of the United States were advised to wear masks, to stay at least one meter apart from other people and to wash their hands frequently. Older people with underlying medical conditions are particularly susceptible to the disease.

Although the first cases of COVID-19 in Florida were reported in Manatee and Hillsborough, 171 people exhibited symptoms of the disease in the first week of January 2020. On April 1, 2020, Governor Ron DeSantis declared a public health emergency, restricting all activities to those considered essential services. The state rescinded all restrictions on businesses and stopped town and city governments from using fines to enforce public health orders, but by the end of fall, Florida had experienced a resurgence in the disease. Between December 31 and January 2, 21,015 new cases began flooding hospitals. By July 2020, 29 percent of all new cases of COVID-19 reported in the United States originated in Florida. Because of Hurricane Isaias, a large number of state-sponsored test sites for COVID-19 were closed between July 20, 2020, and August 5, 2020. On September 25, 2020, Governor DeSantis ordered that all restaurants within the state be reopened. He also prohibited local governments from forcing restaurants to operate at half capacity during the pandemic. With 16,500 deaths reported on October 23, 2020, Florida became fourth in the country in number of fatalities. In May 2021, Governor DeSantis took the

Hollywood Beach, which is usually crowded with tourists, was practically deserted during the early months of the pandemic. *Wikimedia Commons.*

controversial measure of removing the power of school boards and local governments to force students to wear face masks. On April 2, 2021, the governor issued orders prohibiting COVID-19 mitigations. On November 18, 2021, DeSantis signed a bill limiting the power of businesses and local governments to impose vaccine mandates.

By April 19, 2022, approximately 14,343,000 residents of Florida were vaccinated. On January 2, 2023, wordometers.info reported that 7,312,663 Floridians had contracted COVID-19 and that 83,606 Floridians had died from the disease. At the time of this writing, COVID-19 was still claiming lives across the entire United States.

MENINGOCOCCAL OUTBREAK (2022–PRESENT)

All of Florida

Meningococcal disease was first identified as a variant of monkeypox in the United Kingdom in April 2022. In June 2022, the U.S. Centers for Disease

Control and the Florida Department of Health began looking into what they termed "one of the worst outbreaks of meningococcal disease among gay and bisexual men in U.S. history." In Florida, over half of the cases consisted of Hispanic males. Both natives of Florida and visitors to the state have contracted the disease. However, the CDC insists that meningococcal disease can infect anyone.

A bacteria called *Neisseria meningitidis* is believed to be the cause of meningococcal disease, which has been known to take the form of meningitis. According to CNN, the disease can be spread through the sharing of saliva or spit. The disease can also be spread via intimate and lengthy contact, such as kissing. There are two types of meningococcal disease. Meningococcal meningitis is produced when bacteria infect the tissue covering the brain and spinal cord, resulting in inflammation. If *Neisseria meningitidis* infects the bloodstream and causes bleeding in the skin and organs, the type of meningococcal disease is called meningococcemia. Symptoms of

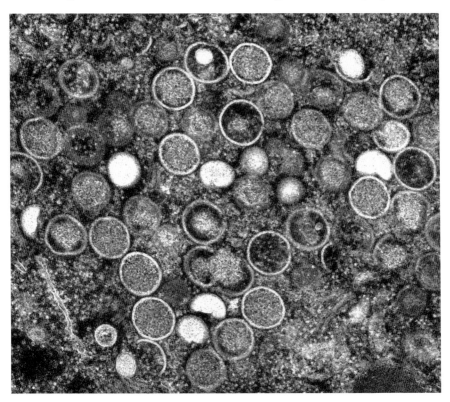

Meningococcal disease is caused by a bacteria called *Neisseria meningitides*. *Wikimedia Commons.*

meningococcal disease include headaches, stiff neck, high fever, nausea, diarrhea, cold hands and feet, rapid breathing and a dark purple rash. According to the CDC, the MenACWY vaccine can be effective as long as treatment begins as soon as the symptoms appear. One out of every ten people who contract the disease dies.

Two types of meningococcal disease can be found in Florida. "Men B" appears primarily among men who have sex with men. College students are also susceptible to a type of meningococcal disease called the Men B because they live in tight quarters, such as dormitories and in fraternities and sororities. A strong proponent of mandating Men B vaccines in Florida colleges and universities is Alicia Stillman, the founder of the Emily Stillman Foundation. Stillman's daughter, Emily, was a college student when she died of meningococcal meningitis 2013. "I believe the state should require two doses of the MenACWY vaccine when graduating from high school," Stillman said.

In Florida, the MenACWY vaccine is available in pharmacies, doctors' offices, local health departments and community health centers. As of this printing, the 2022 meningococcal outbreak was ongoing. According to the CDC, this outbreak was "one of the worst outbreaks" of the disease in U.S. history.

3

GANGSTERS IN PARADISE

THE ASHLEY GANG

The Ashley Gang is one of the least known—and one of the most fascinating—of the Prohibition-era gangs. The progenitor of the gang was Julius Warren "Joe" Ashley. In 1911, he and his wife, Lugenia Clay Ashley, moved to West Palm Beach, where he found work as a railroad officer and a law enforcement officer. On the side, he made moonshine whiskey. The couple raised their nine children in nearby Gomez, where Joe taught his five boys—Bill, Bob, Ed, Frank and John—how to hunt, fish and live off the land. The swamps soon became their second home.

Nineteen-year-old John rose to prominence in the Ashley family in January 1912, when he became the primary suspect in the murder of a trapper named Desoto Tiger, the son of the chief of the Cow Creek Seminoles, Tommy Tiger. Because John was seen in a canoe with Desoto and a load of otter pelts, two deputies were sent to arrest him, but he eluded them in the swamp. John decided to "lay low" in New Orleans for a while. In 1914, he returned to West Palm Beach and surrendered to Sheriff George Baker. John was confident that a jury of people from his community would acquit him of the crime. John was tried in West Palm Beach on July 3, 1914. After a mistrial was declared, John was to be tried a second time in West Palm Beach. However, when he was taken to the Palm Beach County jail, he scaled a ten-foot chicken-wire fence and dashed into the swamp.

Henry Flagler, pictured on the back of a railroad car, founded the Florida East Coast Railway in 1912. The Ashley Gang attempted, unsuccessfully, to rob one of Flagler's trains in 1914. *Wikimedia Commons.*

John was not in his swamp camp for very long before he had formed a gang that included four relatives: his brothers Bob, Ed and Frank and their nephew Hanford Mobley. A bank robber from Chicago named Kid Lowe also became part of the gang. Their first two robberies did not go as planned. Their attempt to rob a Florida East Coast Railroad train was thwarted by a porter who locked all of the cars. After robbing the Bank of Stuart, a bullet fired from Kid Lowe's gun ricocheted off a window frame, breaking John's jaw and blinding his right eye. John was apprehended three hours later and taken to the Dade County jail to await trial for the murder of Desoto Tiger.

On June 2, 1915, John's brother Bob tried, unsuccessfully, to break him out. After shooting Deputy Sheriff Wilber W. Hendrickson, he dropped the deputy's keys in his hurry to escape. Bob then hijacked a delivery truck, but a Miami police officer named John Rhinehart Ribbet attempted to stop him. Both men fired their weapons, and both men died of their wounds.

Afterward, the State of Florida agreed to drop the murder charge in exchange for John agreeing to stand trial for the bank robbery. By the end of the trial, John was found guilty and sentenced to serve seventeen and a half years at the Florida State Penitentiary. His incarceration was cut short when he ran off from the road crew he was assigned to in March 1918 and went back to robbing banks.

The Ashley Gang's criminal enterprises changed drastically when Prohibition became the law of the land on January 17, 1920. Almost overnight, they switched from robbing banks primarily to making moonshine. That same year, John's soon-to-be nemesis Robert C. Baker became Palm Beach sheriff. A few months later, John married Laura Beatrice Upthegrove, who was assigned the job of warning the gang when the police were in the vicinity of their stills.

John's freedom was short-lived. In 1921, he was arrested for driving liquor to Wauchula and was transported to Raiford Prison. During his imprisonment, John's brothers were murdered by a gang of competing rumrunners: Alton Davis, Bo Stokes and Jim White. A few months later, his brothers' murderers "disappeared at sea." Many people in the community believed that John Ashley probably ordered the hit from his prison cell.

In September 1923, John escaped from Raiford Prison and rejoined the Ashley Gang. To supplement their income from their whiskey stills, the gang decided to return to robbing banks. On January 9, 1924, Sheriff Baker made the bold move of raiding the Ashleys' swamp camp with rifles borrowed from the National Guard. During the shoot-out, John witnessed his father being shot in the head. John retaliated by shooting his father's killer. This officer turned out to be Sheriff Robert Baker's cousin Deputy Sheriff Frederick "Fred" Baker. Meanwhile, Laura was shot in the buttocks with shotgun pellets. Her screams distracted the officers long enough for the gang members to flee into the Everglades.

John was still fuming about his father's death when he and his gang robbed the Bank of Pompano. The story goes that John left an unspent bullet with a cashier and told him, "You give that to Sheriff Bob and tell him I got another one just like it waitin' for him if he's man enough to come and get it." Later, when Sheriff Baker received the bullet, he vowed that someday soon, he would take the glass eye that John Ashley was given in prison and wear it as his watch fob.

John Ashley's blood feud with Sheriff Baker grew with every story published in the local newspapers. With his increasing notoriety, John decided to change his modus operandi, robbing banks in Jacksonville with his sister Daisy. The entire time, he was planning to return to Palm Beach County and avenge his father's death. A fateful encounter in a grocery store parking lot between Stuart policeman Oren B. Padgett and John Ashley's brother-in-law George Frances Mario on the morning of November 1, 1924, spelled the beginning of the end for the Ashley Gang. For some unknown reason, Mario had decided to betray his wife's brother by informing Padgett that John Ashley would be driving to Jacksonville that night.

Convinced that Mario was telling the truth about John Ashley's planned trip to Jacksonville, Padgett passed the information along to Sheriff Robert Baker, who contacted the sheriff of St. Lucie County, J.R. Merritt. The men decided the best course of action would be to stretch a heavy chain along the south end of the Sebastian River Bridge and to suspend a red lantern from the center of the chain. Sheriff Baker enlisted the assistance of Palm Beach County deputies Elmer Padgett, Henry Stubbs and L.B. Thomas, whom he sent to the Sebastian River Bridge. Sheriff Merritt added his own two deputies to the ambush party. Sheriff Baker decided not to be present at the bridge, a fact that has puzzled local historians for decades.

Later that day, the lawmen, riding in a black Model T Ford, set up their ambush along both sides of the Sebastian River Bridge at 8:00 p.m. Nothing much happened until 10:30 p.m., when a car appeared out of the darkness and stopped at the bridge. The officers approached the car with their sawed-off shotguns, fully expecting to see the faces of the Ashley Gang staring back at them. To their surprise, the occupants of the car were two young men from Sebastian, Ted R. Miller and Shadrick Odell Davis. Just a few seconds later, another car pulled up behind the first car. Inside were four members of the Ashley Gang: John Ashley, Hanford Mobley, Clarence Middleton and Ray "Shorty" Lynn. While the members of the gang exited their vehicle, Sheriff Merritt rode across the bridge with Miller and Davis to retrieve his car and take the Ashley Gang to the jail in Fort Pierce. As he was passing over the bridge, Sheriff Merritt turned around and noticed that three members of the gang had been handcuffed together and that John Ashley was handcuffed by himself.

According to newspaper coverage of the ambush the next day, the members of the Ashley Gang attacked the lawmen, who defended themselves by shooting all four of them. This was the generally accepted version of the ambush of the Ashley Gang until the 1950s, when a professor at a local junior college interviewed one of the deputies who had participated in the ambush years before. The retired deputy told the deputy that as soon as the car carrying Sheriff Merritt across the bridge was out of sight, the lawmen summarily gunned down the members of the gang. The deputy said that the impulsive decision was made to shoot the lawbreakers because John Ashley had proven over and over again that no jail could hold him. Besides, the gang had murdered three law enforcement officers. It was time that their reign of terror had come to an abrupt end.

After the members of the Ashley Gang were killed, their bodies were transported to Will Fee's Hardware and Mortuary in Fort Pierce. The next morning, the bullet-ridden corpses were displayed on the sidewalk in front of the mortuary, a practice that was carried over from the mid-nineteenth century in America. Eyewitnesses said that John Ashley's glass eye was plucked out of its socket and given to Sheriff Baker. However, after Laura Upthegrove threatened to kill the sheriff if she did not get the eye back, Sheriff Baker returned it to the woman just in time for John Ashley's funeral.

AL CAPONE

Miami and St. Petersburg

Al Capone was born in New York City on January 17, 1899, to Gabriele Capone, a barber, and Teresa Capone, a seamstress. Capone's Italian immigrant parents had seven other children, two of whom ended up working for their brother. Capone's volatile personality got him expelled from school

Al Capone, pictured here in his mug shot, became "Public Enemy No. 1" following the St. Valentine's Day Massacre in Chicago. *Wikimedia Commons.*

at age fourteen for striking a teacher. He worked odd jobs at a bowling alley and a barbershop for a while before becoming a member of local street gangs, like the Five Points Gang. His criminal connections led to his employment as a bouncer in a brothel. After marrying Mae Josephine Coughlin at age nineteen, Capone moved to Chicago, where he became the bodyguard for crime mogul Johnny Torrio, who was making a fortune bootlegging liquor during Prohibition. Capone's role in the organization became even more prominent in 1924 during Torrio's conflict with Dean O'Banion's North Side Gang, which culminated in the murder of the gang's leader on November 10, 1924. Capone soon established business relationships with Canadian bootleggers, which enabled him to smuggle whiskey into the United States. After Torrio was shot several times in 1925, he retired and turned over control of the organization to Capone. He expanded his criminal empire in Chicago by recruiting members of the Black community. Capone reveled in his growing reputation as a nationally known public figure, flaunting his flamboyant lifestyle with custom-made suits, expensive cigars and fine dining. He endeared himself to the general public by supporting local charities and attending baseball games.

Capone's public image was seriously damaged in 1929 when seven members of Bugs Moran's North Side Gang were gunned down, on Capone's orders, in the St. Valentine's Day Massacre. Following the public outcry, newspapers branded him "Public Enemy No. 1." In May 1929, Capone was on his way back to Chicago when he stopped off in Philadelphia. He was arrested outside of a movie theater for carrying an unlicensed .38 revolver. Capone was sentenced to a year in Eastern State Penitentiary, but he served time in a nicely furnished cell. In 1931, Capone was convicted on five counts of tax invasion. The judge sentenced him to serve eleven years in a federal prison. Capone hired a team of lawyers who were Washington-based tax experts to file an appeal with the U.S. Supreme Court, but his appeal was rejected. In May 1932, Capone was transported to the Atlanta U.S. Penitentiary, where he was diagnosed with syphilis, which he had contracted while working as a bodyguard in the Chicago bordello. Charges that he was receiving preferential treatment in prison resulted in his being transferred to

Alcatraz Federal Penitentiary in August 1934. While serving out his sentence in Alcatraz, Capone was diagnosed with syphilis of the brain. Because his behavior was becoming increasingly erratic, Capone spent most of his last year in Alcatraz in the prison infirmary. On January 6, 1930, Capone was sent to the Correctional Institution at Terminal Island in California so that he could serve out his sentence for contempt. However, his wife arranged with the court to gain her husband's early release because of his deteriorating mental condition, and he was paroled on November 16, 1939.

Capone was treated for syphilis at Union Memorial Hospital soon after his release from prison. The penicillin injections he received there extended his life but did not cure the disease. After leaving the hospital, Capone returned to Florida to spend what time he had left in his Palm Island mansion. Capone died of a heart attack in his mansion on January 25, 1947, surrounded by his family. He was buried in Mount Olive Cemetery in Chicago. Three years later, his body was exhumed and reinterred, along with the remains of his father, Gabriele, and his brother Frank in Mount Carmel Cemetery, Illinois.

Al Capone died in his Miami mansion on January 25, 1947. *Wikimedia Commons*.

Al Capone's connection to St. Petersburg is largely based on rumor and speculation. According to a history published by the Shore Acres Civic Association, Capone bought a house on what is now Venetian Boulevard in 1926. The ten-room house afforded residents a view in all directions, and its location would have been ideal for smuggling liquor across the bay. The presence of engraved fish above the fireplace could be a reference to a phrase used by mobsters at the time—"Sleeping with the fishes"—that refers to dumping corpses in bodies of water. Many locals believe that Capone built the house either as a home for his mother or as a bordello for his girlfriend. No evidence exists supporting either allegation. Fred Palsey, author of *Al Capone: Biography of a Self-Made Man*, wrote that Capone visited St. Petersburg in 1928, but the police made him feel welcome by meeting him at the trains station and following him around town. In an article published in the *Northeast Journal*, historian Will Michaels contests Palsey's assertion on the grounds that such a visit by Capone would have been a "newsworthy event."

According to an article published in the February 10, 1931 edition of the *St. Petersburg Times*, Capone traveled to St. Petersburg to visit his former mentor, Johnny Torrio. While he was there, Capone is believed to have visited the sponge industry in 1931 with five other people, one of whom was a woman, and spent two nights at the Royal Palm Hotel. According to an article published in the *Times* in 1992, Capone and his henchmen also stayed at the Royal Palm Hotel in 1926. He is rumored to have registered under "A. Brown," an alias that he often used. In the same article, Capone was reported to have traveled to Tarpon Springs on February 9, 1931, where he "spent several days." At one time, the website of the Don Cesar Hotel stated that Al Capone once stayed at the hotel during one of his visits to St. Petersburg, but that statement has been removed. Will Michaels also questioned the persistent rumors that Al Capone had extensive real estate investments in St. Petersburg because, at the time, Capone was well-off financially and did not need to invest there. While it is true that St. Petersburg certainly did attract a parade of celebrities during its boom era in the 1920s, like F. Scott Fitzgerald, John Philip Sousa, Clarence Darrow, Will Rogers and Babe Ruth, little hard evidence suggests that the city was a "second home" to Al Capone.

On the other hand, Al Capone really did purchase a fourteen-room mansion on Palm Island in March 1928. The previous owner of the estate was beer mogul August Anheuser Busch. Capone paid $40,000 for the mansion. Over the years, he made over $200,000 worth of improvements, including a seven-foot-high wall, a gatehouse, a cabana, searchlights and a coral rock grotto. The seven-bedroom, seven-bathroom home is a 7,500-square-foot Spanish-Colonial mansion. It also has a private beach and a beautiful view of Biscayne Bay. The mansion's 30-by-60-foot swimming pool was reputed to be the largest privately owned pool in the entire state. In 1929, Al Capone was in Miami, meeting with an assistant district attorney shortly after the St. Valentine's Day Massacre. Developer Todd Michael Glaser's announcement that he was going to demolish the mansion, which he and his business partner had purchased for $10.75 million, angered historical preservationists in the state and prompted an online petition that garnered more than twenty-five thousand signatures. Because of the petition, the developers withdrew their application to the local design review board to have the mansion razed. In 2021, Capone's mansion was purchased for $15.5 million and saved from demolition.

THE BARKER-KARPIS GANG

The woman who came to be known as "Ma" Barker was born Arizona Clark on October 8, 1873, in Ash Grove, Missouri. Her Scotch-Irish parents, John and Emaline Clark, were poor. According to legend, Arizona saw the James Gang ride through town when she was very young. According to the website Biography.com, this sighting ignited a desire for adventure within her. In 1892, she married George E. Barker, a tenant farmer. The couple raised their four sons—Herman, Lloyd, Arthur and Fred—in Aurora, Missouri. "Kate," as she was known at this time, raised her family in poverty. Around 1904, the family moved to Webb City, Missouri. Her sons began breaking the law at an early age, primarily because their mother refused to discipline them. In 1910, Herman Barker was arrested on the charge of highway robbery. Soon after the family moved to Tulsa, Oklahoma, in 1915, her sons began associating with young lawbreakers near the Old Lincoln Forsythe School and eventually joined up with the Central Park Gang. By 1923, all four boys were incarcerated, either in jail or in reformatories. Kate found herself spending most of her time trying to get her sons released. On August 29, 1927, Herman shot a policeman in the mouth following a robbery in Wichita, Kansas, and shot himself to avoid prosecution. By 1928, George had left Kate, claiming that she was having affairs with other men. He also refused to stand up for Lloyd after he got arrested. Between 1928 and 1930, Kate was alone, living in

Arthur "Doc" Barker was incarcerated on Alcatraz Island in 1935. His friend Alvin "Creepy" Karpis was imprisoned there between 1936 and 1862. *Wikimedia Commons.*

a shack. In 1930, she took up with an unemployed man named Arthur W. Dunlop, but she was still poverty-stricken.

Kate's life changed in 1931 when her youngest son, Fred, was paroled from Lansing Prison in Kansas. He returned to Tulsa in 1931 with a friend he had made in prison, Alvin Karpis. The two men used Kate's shack as a hideout between robberies. Kate became a wanted criminal in December 1931 after Fred and Karpis shot Sheriff C.R. Kelly following the robbery of a department store in West Plains, Missouri. At the time, the sheriff was getting two tires fixed at a garage. Soon thereafter, a wanted poster was distributed naming Ma Barker as an accomplice. Other crimes followed, including the robbery of the Northwestern National Bank in Minneapolis on March 29, 1932. The Barker-Karpis gang got away with $250,000 in cash. The gang's notoriety escalated after Barker's son Doc was paroled for murder in September 1932. The Barker-Karpis gang robbed the Third Northwestern National Bank in Minneapolis in December 1932, but the men got into a shootout with police, leaving two officers and one civilian dead.

In the summer of 1933, the Barker-Karpis Gang branched out into kidnapping. William A. Hamm Jr., the president of the Theodore Hamm Brewing Company, had just left his office when four men grabbed him from behind and pushed him into a waiting car. They then transported Hamm to Wisconsin, where he was forced to sign several ransom notes. Afterward, the men drove to Bensenville, Illinois, to await payment. After the gang received the ransom money, they released Hamm in Wyoming, Minnesota. The men then returned to Chicago, where they planned to launder the ransom money. In September 1933, the FBI was able to remove the gang's fingerprints from the ransom notes.

Flush with the success of their first kidnapping, the Barker-Karpis gang kidnapped a wealthy banker named Edward George Bremer Jr. in St. Paul, Minnesota, on January 17, 1934. He was released three weeks later after his family paid a ransom of $200,000. However, Arthur "Doc" Barker unwittingly gave the police a break when he left a fingerprint on a gas can found along the road.

The Barker-Karpis Gang's reign of terror came to a violent end in 1935. On January 8, 1935, Doc Barker was arrested. When the arresting officers were searching him, they found a map and letters, one of which made a reference to a famous alligator living in Lake Weir, Florida, "Ole Joe." The lake was only a mile away from a cottage near Ocklawaha, where Fred and Ma Barker were living. Using the alias Mrs. T.C. "Kate" Blackburn, Ma Barker had rented the house from Carson Bradford in late 1934, stating that she and her sons need a place to recover from the cold winters up North.

At 5:30 a.m. on January 16, 1935, FBI agents converged on the Bradford house. The special agent in charge ordered the occupants—Fred and Ma Barker—to surrender. Fifteen minutes later, someone inside the house said, "All right, go ahead." Suddenly, the silence was broken by the rat-a-tat-tat of machine gun fire from inside the house. A furious shoot-out ensued between the Barkers and the lawmen. After a while, a crowd of spectators gathered around the house. Four hours later, gunfire from inside the house ceased. As the lawmen cautiously entered the house, they were relieved to find that both Fred and Ma Barker were dead. Fred had been shot multiple times. Ma was shot only once. A search of the house turned up two .45-caliber automatic pistols, two Thompson submachine guns, a Browning 12-gauge automatic shotgun, a .33-caliber Winchester rifle, a Remington 12-gauge pump shotgun and a .380-caliber Colt automatic pistol.

The bodies of Fred Barker and Ma Barker were put on display for a while before relatives finally claimed them on October 1, 1935. Ma and Fred Barker were buried alongside Herman Barker at Williams Timberhill Cemetery in Welch, Oklahoma.

The villainous image of Ma Barker as the ruthless leader of her brood of bloodthirsty killers has come into question over the years. The FBI's portrayal of the matriarch of the Barker family as "Bloody Mama" and the ringleader of the gang is unsupported by the evidence, which suggests that she probably knew of her sons' crimes but had no hand in planning them. Years later, Alvin Karpis, who was the actual leader of the gang, described her as "an old-fashioned homebody from the Ozarks." Nevertheless, the FBI's depiction of Ma Barker as a homicidal outlaw has been perpetuated in films like *Guns Don't Argue* (1957), *Ma Barker's Killer Brood* (1960) and *Bloody Mama* (1970).

In 2016, the two-story home where Ma and Fred Barker made their last stand was slated for demolition. However, volunteers from the area had the house placed on a floating barge and moved from Lake Weir to Carney Island Recreation and Conservation Area. Following several restoration efforts, the historic home has been converted into a house museum. Some bullet holes from the gunfight can still be seen in the walls and furniture.

4

LEGENDARY DEATHS

THE BERMUDA TRIANGLE

The Bermuda Triangle, also known as the Devil's Triangle, is a section of the Atlantic Ocean bounded by Miami, Florida; San Juan, Puerto Rico; and Bermuda, where an unusually large number of boats and aircraft have been lost. Some ships were discovered abandoned in the Bermuda Triangle for no apparent reason. Estimates of the total area of the Bermuda Triangle range from 500,000 square miles to 1,510,000 square miles. The floor of the Bermuda Triangle is littered with countless wrecks. Because no one knows for certain why so many people have been lost in the Bermuda Triangle, it has been enveloped in an aura of mystery for over five hundred years.

The first notable report of strange phenomena in the Bermuda Triangle was made by Christopher Columbus. When he passed through the area in the sixteenth century, Columbus claimed that the stars appeared to move about in the sky. He and his crew also observed a strange light moving up and down on the horizon before disappearing completely. The most startling occurrence in the Bermuda Triangle, according to Columbus, was a large, glowing object that shot out of the water and soared into the night sky.

One of the best-known disappearances in the Bermuda Triangle in the nineteenth century took place on January 31, 1880, when the HMS *Atalanta* left port in Royal Naval Dockyard, Bermuda, for Falmouth, England. Two weeks later, the ship vanished. Most people blamed the loss of the ship on a powerful storm or its largely untrained crew. Some people believed that the training ship HMS *Eurydice*, which disappeared two years earlier, was somehow connected to the fate of the *Atalanta*. People across the world suspected that some mysterious force within the Bermuda Triangle may have been responsible.

The disappearance of the 543-foot-long navy cargo ship USS *Cyclops* entailed the largest loss of life in the history of the U.S. Navy unrelated to wartime. The *Cyclops* left Barbados fully loaded with ten thousand tons of manganese ore in 1918. The navy lost all contact with the vessel after March 4, 1918, between Barbados and the Chesapeake Bay. The ship did not send out an SOS signal, even though it had the equipment. No trace of the *Cyclops* was ever found. Explanations for the loss of the ship and its 309-man crew included German warships and fierce storms. However, an examination of German submarine records revealed that no German subs were active in the area at that time. In recent years, nautical experts have blamed overloading for the sinking of the *Cyclops*.

The most famous disappearance of aircraft over the Bermuda Triangle took place on December 5, 1945. Five Navy Grumman TBM-3 Avenger torpedo bombers left base at Fort Lauderdale at 2:10 p.m. The flight leader, Lieutenant Charles Taylor, had over 2,500 hours flying time. Their mission involved practice bombing runs on a target hulk 56 miles away. The planes would then fly 160 miles to the east and 40 miles to the north before returning to the base. After completing the bombing runs at 3:15 p.m., Lieutenant Taylor radioed the following message to the Tower: "This is an emergency. We seem to be off course. We cannot see land…Repeat… We cannot see land." He ended his message by stating: "We can't be sure of any direction—even the ocean doesn't look as it should." At 3:50 p.m., flight instructor Lieutenant Cox made radio contact with Lieutenant Taylor, who said he could not find the way back to Fort Lauderdale. Lieutenant Cox advised Lieutenant Taylor that if he was in the Keys, he should continue northward until he reached the Fort Lauderdale Naval Air Station. Actually, Lieutenant Taylor was in the Bahamas, not the Keys. The tower picked up conversations from the planes in Flight 19. The pilots complained that that every gyro and magnetic compass in the planes was "going crazy." According to some reports, the last words from Flight 19 were "It looks like we are…" Several rescue craft left the base in search of Flight 19. One of these planes, a PBM Mariner, vanished as well, although a tanker reported seeing an explosion and a large oil slick. A naval investigation concluded that Lieutenant Taylor was responsible for the loss of the aircraft. However,

Flight 19, which vanished on December 5, 1945, was the most famous disappearance of aircraft over the Bermuda Triangle. *Wikimedia Commons.*

following pressure from Taylor's family, the navy changed the reason for the disaster to "causes or reasons unknown."

Two more high-profile disappearances of planes occurred in 1948. On January 29, 1948, a converted Lancashire bomber with a crew of six, the *Star Tiger*, vanished while on flight from the Azores to Bermuda. This tragedy was particularly noteworthy because one of the twenty-five passengers was

On December 28, 1948, a DC-3 passenger plane, like the one pictured here, disappeared over the Bermuda Triangle while flying from San Juan to Miami. *Wikimedia Commons.*

Sir Arthur Cunningham, a World War II British air marshal. Then on December 28, 1948, a DC-3 passenger plane flying from San Juan to Miami never made it. Thirty-two passengers and crew members were on board at the time.

Over the years, a number of natural explanations for the loss of life in the Bermuda Triangle have been proposed, including compass problems, violent storms and massive bubbles of methane gas called hydrates. Theorists unwilling to accept mundane explanations have suggested that UFOs, a time/space warp and even the lost continent of Atlantis could be responsible. The fact is that thousands of planes and ships pass through the Bermuda Triangle every year with no problems at all.

Calvin C. Phillips's Mausoleum

Tallahassee

Biographical details about architect Calvin C. Phillips are sketchy, at best. According to the article "Calvin C. Phillips Tallahassee's Mysterious Recluse," he was born in New York in 1834. In the 1860 census, he was listed as a master carpenter. At the time, he was living with his wife and daughter in Schroeppel, New York. By 1865, he and his family had moved to Palermo, New York. In an advertisement published the next year, he stated that he was a "millwright" and "builder." In the 1870 census, he was listed as a master carpenter with a wife and two children. In 1876, he designed the Liberty Stove Works Building at the Philadelphia Centennial Exposition of 1876. Phillips received a patent for the "Vertical Grinding Mill" on January 5, 1878. In 1879, Phillips was awarded a medal by the Pennsylvania State Agricultural Society for his design for a portable gristmill. According to the 1880 census, he was living with his wife and daughter in Philadelphia. His occupation was listed in the census as "Machinist." In 1889, Phillips was awarded a bronze medal at the Universal Exposition of 1889 in Paris. By 1900, Phillips and his wife had separated. Soon after, Phillips took up residence in Tallahassee, Florida, in 1907. That same year, he purchased a plot in Oakland Cemetery near the corner of Brevard and North Bronough Streets. While living in Tallahassee, Phillips was reputed to be a recluse whose only confidant was his lawyer, State Senator William C. Hodge. In the 1985 editorial "The Tale of a Man Obsessed with Time," retired governor LeRoy Collins said, "No one recalls ever seeing Phillips in a bank, post office, church, school or other place where groups of people normally would gather." Phillips died in Tallahassee on November 19, 1919.

Calvin C. Phillips is said to have built his twenty-foot-high mausoleum, the largest mausoleum in Oaklawn Cemetery, with his own hands. *Wikimedia Commons.*

As often happens, legend has stepped in to fill in the gaps in Phillips's biography. Locals say that not long after arriving in Tallahassee, Phillips began work on his mausoleum. It is said that he spent years designing and building the twenty-foot-tall structure with his own hands. People walking past the cemetery said that on exceedingly hot days, Phillips slept on a cot inside the mausoleum to escape the heat. The finished product is a fascinating melding of Doric, Indian, Greek and Roman architectural styles. The tomb's most striking feature is its minaret-shaped dome. According to legend, after completing his mausoleum—the largest in Oaklawn Cemetery—Phillips hired a coffin-maker to make him a cherrywood casket. After it was finished, he had the casket delivered to his mausoleum. After the workmen left, he climbed into the coffin, folded his arms and died. In another version of the story, he asked that he be buried sitting upright.

The strange story of Calvin C. Phillips's death and interment does not end here. In April 2000, Phillips's skull was stolen from his mausoleum. As of this printing, his skull has not been returned. Perhaps this is the reason why the unquiet spirit of Calvin C. Phillips has been seen perched on topic of his mausoleum.

THE CASTILLO DE SAN MARCOS'S DARK SECRET

St. Augustine

Legends of ill-fated lovers have been told and retold for centuries, not only because they tug at our heartstrings, but also because they resonate with the cost of violating the norms of society. The Castillo de San Marcos was constructed in 1672 to protect the city of St. Augustine. Built of long-lasting coquina stone, the Castillo de San Marcos is the oldest existing permanent seacoast fortification in the continental United States. During its three-hundred-plus-year history, the fort has survived several wars, countless pirate attacks, battles and storms. Another element of the fort that has withstood the passing of time is the tragic tale of two ill-fated lovers.

In 1784, the fortress was under the command of a Spanish officer named Garcia Marti. He was married to a beautiful woman named Delores, who was known to wear a particularly strong perfume. Colonel Marti suspected that his wife and a dashing young officer named Captain Manuel Abela were having an affair. When both of them turned up missing, the colonel

According to legend, the commander of the Castillo de San Marcos, Colonel Garcia Marti, chained his wife and her lover to a dungeon wall. *Wikimedia Commons*.

explained that he had sent Captain Abela on a secret mission and that his wife had taken ill and was sent to her aunt's house. The actual fate of the couple did not come to light until 1833, when an American officer detected a hollow sound in one of the walls of the dungeon area. He removed a brick and was instantly overcome by the scent of strong perfume. Workers soon made a grisly discovery: a hidden room containing two skeletons—male and female—who were chained to the wall. It is believed that this was Garcia Marti's way of punishing his adulterous wife and her handsome lover. Today, the forlorn spirit of Delores Marti is said to roam the grounds of the Castillo wearing a white dress. Some visitors claim to have smelled her perfume. For years, people have also said that when they placed their ear against the stone wall of the room where there the lovers were found, they could hear the moans of the slowly dying couple.

DEATH BY ANTHRAX

Robert Stevens was a photojournalist who traveled to South Florida from Great Britain in the 1970s to work for the *National Inquirer*. By 2001, he had become a naturalized U.S. citizen, living in Lantana, Florida, and working for a different tabloid, the *Sun*, in Boca Raton. Both tabloids were owned by

American Media Inc. and housed in the same building. On October 2, 2002, he and his wife, Maureen, were driving home from Charlotte, North Carolina, when he developed flu-like symptoms: nausea and difficulty breathing. Maureen drove him to the John F. Kennedy Medical Center in Palm Beach, Florida. At first, doctors diagnosed Stevens with meningitis. However, when he died four days later, the cause of death was listed as anthrax inhalation, making him the first person to die of the disease in twenty-five years.

Anthrax, an infectious disease caused by rod-shaped bacteria known as *Bacillus anthracis*, can be found naturally in soil. Human beings can become infected through close contact with animals. Because Stevens was an avid fisherman, his doctors originally assumed that he had contracted the disease in North Carolina while fishing in a creek. However, investigators from the FBI suspected that he might have been one of several journalists who received letters containing anthrax in a powdery form in the mail. As soon as spores were discovered on Stevens's keyboard in his office, the entire American Media building was evacuated.

Later, the FBI determined that five letters containing a white or brown powder laced with anthrax spores had been mailed to ABC News, CBS News and NBC News in New York and to the *National Inquirer* in Boca Raton. Scientists found that all of the spores in the letters belonged to the Ames strain. Tracing the strain to the U.S. Army Medical Research Institute of Infectious Diseases eventually led investigators to a microbiologist named Bruce Edward Ivins. He became a prime suspect after the FBI learned that he had worked a number of late nights just before the letters were sent to the news outlets. When investigators interrogated Ivins in March 2005, he was unable to provide a satisfactory explanation for his overtime hours. Just as FBI agents were about to arrest Ivins in 2008, he died by suicide. It turned out that Ivins had a history of making threats against his coworkers and that he had been treated by a psychiatrist.

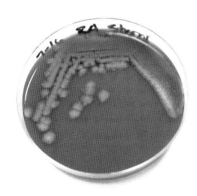

Anthrax spores, like the ones used to infect journalists in Florida, are naturally found in soil. *Pixnio.*

Robert Stevens was one of five people who died of anthrax inhalation in 2001. In 2003, Stevens's family filed a lawsuit, claiming that the federal government had not adequately secured its supply of anthrax. In 2011, the court awarded Maureen Stevens $2.5 million.

Death by Suitcase

Winter Park

In February 2020, Sarah Boone (forty-two) and her boyfriend, Jorge Torres (also forty-two), were in their Winter Park apartment doing puzzles. After drinking several glasses of chardonnay, the couple decided to play hide-and-seek. They hid in different parts of the apartment before deciding that it would be "fun" if Sarah zipped Jorge up in a suitcase. Once he was inside the suitcase, Sarah went upstairs and went to bed. She assumed that he would eventually get out of the suitcase, even though only a couple of fingers were sticking out of the zipper, and would join her in bed later on. At eleven o'clock the next morning, the telephone rang, waking her up. Sarah expected to find Jorge sitting at his computer. When she was unable to find Jorge anywhere in the apartment, she walked over to the suitcase and was shocked to find that he had stopped breathing. She then dialed 911 and told the dispatcher that her boyfriend was dead and that she thought he had had an aneurysm.

When the police arrived at her apartment. Jorge's body was lying on the floor by a suitcase. His body was bruised, and he had a small cut on his lip. After listening to Sarah's story, the police searched the apartment and collected evidence, including her cellphone. Upon examination of the phone, the police discovered that Sarah had recorded video of the "game" she and her boyfriend were playing. The camera was pointed at the suitcase during the entire recording. Torres could clearly be seen pushing on the sides of suitcase, pleading with Sarah to let him out. At one point in the recording, Sarah said, "For everything you've done to me." In response to his plea that he could not breathe, Sarah could be heard saying, "That's what I feel like when you cheat on me." Sarah had completely forgotten that she had made the recording.

The autopsy revealed that Jorge had died of asphyxiation and that he was severely beaten. Sarah was placed in jail in Orange County without bond. She was charged with second-degree murder.

Spontaneous Human Combustion

St. Petersburg

On July 2, 1951, Pansy Carpenter stopped by the apartment of her sixty-seven-year-old tenant, Mary Reeser, to deliver a telegram at 8:07 p.m. She knocked on the door, but no one answered. When Carpenter grabbed the doorknob, she released it immediately because of the intense heat. Alarmed, she called over to two painters who were working across the street. When the men opened the door and noticed the blackened walls, they told Carpenter to call the police. When the police and firefighters entered the apartment, the first thing they noticed was that even though the apartment was very hot, they could find little evidence of a fire. When they found Reeser's corpse sitting in the remains of a chair, they had the shock of their lives. With the exception of part of her skull, which had shrunken to the size of a teacup; her left foot in a satin slipper; and part of her backbone, her body was completely cremated. Most of the small objects near the body had been melted by the heat, including plastic light switches. The carpet was burned in an area three feet in diameter. Only the springs of Reeser's chair and two legs of a small end table survived the fire. Although two candles placed near the window had melted, their wicks were intact. Newspapers by a nearby table were not singed at all. No fuses had been blown, and the electric current was still working. The apartment showed the effects of extreme heat on the ceiling and walls approximately four feet from the floor. The men could not explain how a human body could be so destroyed and the fire confined to such a small space without causing damage to the structure of the building and the furniture in the room.

J.R. Reichert, the St. Petersburg chief of police, was so baffled by what had transpired in the apartment on 1200 Cherry Street that he mailed boxes of evidence to the FBI, including parts of Reeser's chair, rubble from the wall and a small portion of the rug. Because of the mysterious condition of the apartment and the body itself, investigators considered the possibility that Reeser might have been a victim of spontaneous combustion, which is believed to occur when chemical reactions inside the body cause it to burst into flame without an external heat source. Despite the fact that cases of spontaneous human combustion have been reported since the seventeenth century, most scientists are still not convinced that it really exists.

Mary Reeser's death became one of the first cases of potential spontaneous human combustion to be investigated by national law enforcement. Investigators at the FBI concluded that Reeser had fallen into a deep sleep because of the sedatives she had taken that night. Most likely, she was smoking when she fell asleep, and her own body fat—she was overweight—ignited the flames. Therefore, Reeser did not die from spontaneous human combustion. The exact cause of her death, however, is still a mystery.

5

NATURAL CATASTROPHES

FLORIDA KEYS HURRICANE (1906)

Ever since the media and meteorologists began recording the dates and strength of hurricanes in Florida in 1851, tropical cyclonic activity has made landfall in the state at least once per year. In fact, most of the major hurricanes that have been recorded since 1851 have passed through either Florida or Texas. Meteorologists believe that Florida has become a "hurricane hub" because the peninsula tends to bring in hurricanes from the east to the west. Although Florida's hurricanes have been the costliest in terms of loss of life and property, the most powerful storms as of this writing were Hurricanes Katrina and Camille and the 1780 San Calixto Storm.

Even though Florida has definitely had more than its share of hurricanes, the state actually reports only one major hurricane approximately every ten years. The first of these killer storms hit Florida in 1906. The Florida Key Hurricane (Category 2) first made landfall in Central America. After becoming a Category 3 hurricane on October 17, the center of the storm passed east of Havana during the night. On the morning of October 18, the hurricane blew over south Florida before heading north and weakened east of South Carolina. When it curved south–southwestward, the hurricane passed over Florida once again.

The destruction inflicted on Florida was considerable. Water surged through the streets of Miami. Strong winds flattened houses in the city and completely destroyed churches and the jail, forcing the evacuation of the prisoners. The streets of St. Augustine were inundated as well. Ships also bore the brunt of the fury of the hurricane. Fierce winds and powerful waves destroyed the *Elmora*, *Campbell* and *Sara* near the Isle of Pines. Around seventy passengers aboard the steamers *St. Lucia* and *Peerless* lost their lives in the storm. Telephone lines were knocked down south of Jupiter.

The Florida East Coast Railway sustained the heaviest damage during the hurricane. In 1906, entrepreneur Henry Flagler was building a spur from Miami to Key West. Of the approximately 135 people who were killed, 104 died on the railroad's Houseboat No. 4. Waves washed an untold number of railway workers out of flatboats and barges into the sea. The steamer *Jenny* rescued 42 workers. The railway's financial losses amounted to $200,000. Because of the time required to repair equipment, construction of the railway was pushed back for a year. Farmers, especially pineapple growers, suffered heavy losses. Six workers on plantations in the Keys perished in the storm. The hurricane moved West toward South Carolina, but the next day, the tropical storm struck Jackson and passed through the rest of the state.

FLORIDA KEYS HURRICANE (1909)

Thirteen tropical cyclones came out of the 1909 Atlantic hurricane season: nine of them were tropical storms, and six became hurricanes, four of which were major hurricanes. One of these major hurricanes—the 1909 Florida Keys hurricane—severely damaged Cuba and the Florida Keys. It was a tropical storm on October 6 when it made its first appearance in the Caribbean Sea off the shore of Colombia on October 6. It was a Category 1 hurricane when it passed southwest of Jamaica on October 8.

On October 10, the hurricane made landfall in Key West. Its eighty-five-mile-per-hour winds devastated half of the city, knocking down telephone and light poles along Duval Street. Seven churches and nine cigar factories were demolished as well. Several horses and firemen were killed when two engine houses at the fire department collapsed. Strong winds lifted the roof off the First National Bank and heavily damaged the post office. Along the shore, the huge waves drowned large numbers of fishermen and their families; they also damaged hundreds of ships. Damages in Key West totaled $2 million. To prevent looting, the mayor of Key West, Joseph N. Fogarty,

The beached boat depicted in this photograph is just one of hundreds of vessels destroyed in Key West by the 1909 Florida Keys Hurricane. *Wikimedia Commons.*

not only declared martial law, but he also appealed to the federal government to send in the armed forces.

Key West was not the only one of the Florida Keys to feel the fury of the hurricane. The winds were so powerful on Sand Key that the staff at the Weather Bureau were forced to abandon the office. The one-hundred-mile-per-hour blasts blew away the anemometer cup, cracked two windows at the top of the lighthouse and knocked down the signal tower and every tree on the island. Four feet of water surged through the island, washing away the Weather Bureau building and the outhouses. The Florida East Coast Railway was interrupted by nature's wrath. At Boca Chica and Sugarloaf Keys, the camps for railway workers were blown apart. When the tugboat *Sybil* wrecked at Bahia Honda Key, twelve people died.

The 1909 Key West Hurricane also raged through mainland Florida. In Miami, the storm ripped the roofs off warehouses, homes and an assortment of other buildings. The March Villa Hotel, which had just been completed a few weeks before, was heavily damaged. Most of the damage in Miami took the form of downed trees. A train traveling along a spur of the Florida East Coast Railway was delayed for four hours when sections of the track were washed out around Hallandale. The rainfall was so heavy at Deerfield that all of the crops were destroyed.

On October 11, the hurricane struck Pinar del Rio Province in Cuba before striking the Straits of Florida. Marathon, Florida, was buffeted with 115-mile-per-hour winds. The timekeeper at Marathon drowned in the waves. The next day, the storm was reduced to a Category 2 hurricane when its 105-mile-per-hour winds struck Grand Bahama and the Abaco Islands. It became a tropical storm on October 12. In Florida, it was responsible for $3 million in damage and thirty-four deaths.

CUBA HURRICANE (1910)

On October 9, 1910, a tropical cyclone began to develop in in the southern Caribbean. When the storm moved north, it gained strength. By October 12, it had attained hurricane status. The next day, the storm was moving toward Cuba. Just before it reached the western tip of Cuba on October 14, it had become a Category 4 hurricane. The storm lost speed as it passed over the Gulf of Mexico. On October 16, the hurricane turned northward with 150-mile-per-hour winds toward western Cuba, where strong winds destroyed crops, flooded towns and cities and did substantial damage to plantations, like the tobacco farms of Vuetta Abajo. The Pina del Rio province suffered the greatest losses in terms of property and people. A large number of ships were wrecked by the wind and waves. By the time the hurricane had moved on toward Florida, approximately one hundred people were dead and $1 million worth of property was destroyed.

On October 17, the hurricane's 110-mile-per-hour wind gusts destroyed docks in Key West. Rising waters flooded the Weather Bureau's basement. An entertainment venue called La Brisa was completely destroyed. On the southern and western shores of Key West, winds and waves washed a number of homes off their foundations and into the sea.

Tampa began feeling the effects of the hurricane as it progressed westward. Winds were so powerful that they blew most of the water out of Tampa Bay. From Flamingo to Cape Romono, the surf battered homes and buildings, forcing many residents to seek shelter in the tops of trees. High winds blew the roof off some houses and knocked others off their foundations from Tampa to Jacksonville.

The effects of the hurricane were not as catastrophic on the eastern coast of Florida. Between October 14 and October 18, rain fell every day, flooding creeks and flat woods. However, because the sea was so low, officials were

La Brisa, the pleasure pavilion of the Key West Electric Company, was destroyed by the hurricane of 1910 on October 17, 1910. *Wikimedia Commons.*

This structure owned by the United Wireless Telegraph Company in Key West was turned completely upside down by the hurricane of 1910. *Wikimedia Commons.*

able to open the inlet and reduce the water level. Trees were blown down in and around Jupiter and Lemon City. Except for some damage to cocks and boathouses, the east coast did not suffer as much as other parts of Florida. Before dissipating on October 23, the hurricane moved north to Georgia and South Carolina. Most of the damage in cities like Savannah was caused by high tides.

FLORIDA KEYS HURRICANE (1919)

The storm that has come to be known as one of the worst hurricanes to ever strike the Gulf Coast started out as a tropical depression off the Bahamas and began to move west through the Caribbean and the Gulf of Mexico. Within one day, it reached Category 3 status. One day later, it strengthened to a Category 4 hurricane with wind speeds of 140–50 miles per hour. By the time it reached Florida on September 9, the storm had the power to destroy everything in its path, remaining a Category 4 hurricane through September 13. It moved slowly, averaging around 4 miles per hour. While the hurricane passed through the Florida Straits, it sank ten ships, killing 500 people, 488 of whom died aboard the huge Spanish vessel *Valbanera*. Eight former navy patrol yachts were lost in the hurricane, including USS *Helena I*. Although most of the residents of Key West managed to escape with their lives, many of their houses were torn apart. Property losses were over $2 million. Almost every structure—homes, churches, schools, stores and so on—had some sort of damage. South Florida, on the other hand, was not nearly as severely affected by the hurricane. The wind speed of the hurricane never exceeded 26 miles per hour as it moved to the southern part of the city. Property damage in Miami was minor as well, although the rough seas destroyed seventeen houseboats and a small boat in Biscayne Bay.

On September 14, what was now a Category 3 hurricane ravaged Texas between Brownsville and Corpus Christi with winds reaching 115 miles per hour. The highest storm surge on record struck the Corpus Christi area at 16 feet. Some of the piles of debris in the city were 17 feet high. Downton Corpus Christi was littered with 1,400 bales of cotton and large stockpiles of lumber. Approximately 1,500 cattle were driven into the sea and drowned by the storm. In the North Beach area, hundreds of people were washed into Nueces Bay along with their houses. The death toll was listed as 283, but this body count included only those people who could be positively identified.

This is one of many houses completely torn apart by the 1919 Florida Keys Hurricane. *Wikimedia Commons.*

Most historians agree that it is more likely that 600 people died in their sleep, mostly because many living on the Texas coast did not prepare for the oncoming storm. Six years after the storm, the City of Corpus Christi built a breakwater. The entire seawall was completed in 1940.

Of the six to nine hundred people who lost their lives in the hurricane, five hundred of them were aboard the ten ships that were sunk. At the time, this was the second-strongest hurricane to make landfall in the United States. It was the sixth most intense hurricane in U.S. history.

OKEECHOBEE HURRICANE (1928)

One of the most power hurricanes ever to make landfall in the United States was first sighted on 900 miles east of Guadeloupe on September 10, 1928. The storm had reached Category 3 status by the time it approached the Caribbean. On September 12, 1928, it reached Guadeloupe. The next day, it made landfall in Puerto Rico as a Category 5 hurricane with 160-mile-per-hour winds. It was the first Category 5 hurricane in the Atlantic basin. Because the citizens of Puerto Rico were made aware of the impending hurricane well ahead of time, the death toll was low: 312. Warnings on radio broadcasts were responsible for the fact that no ships were lost. By the time the hurricane passed over the Bahamas, it was a Category 4 hurricane. Although property losses were great, the loss of life in Puerto Rico was minimal. In fact, the only deaths were the 18 people who drowned when their sloop was lost at sea around Ambergris.

However, the damage in Florida was much worse. While it is true that Miami, Hollywood and Fort Lauderdale emerged from the storm relatively unscathed, many buildings from Pompano Beach to Jupiter were heavily damaged by the strong winds and the storm surge. Property damage in Palm Beach amounted to several million dollars, but only twenty-six people died, mostly because the residents were given adequate warning.,

The situation was worse in the heavily populated coast of Lake Okeechobee—it was catastrophic. On September 16, 1928, residents were given adequate warning, but when the hurricane did not arrive at the predicted time, most of them returned to their homes. Prior to the hurricane, Lake Okeechobee was higher than normal, mostly because a thunderstorm had struck the lake's north side in August 1938. By mid-September, forty-seven inches of rainfall had soaked the ground. The water easily surged over the four-foot dikes at the south side of the lake, flooding hundreds of square miles, reaching a depth in some places of over twenty feet. The flimsy houses, most of which were occupied, were forced off their foundations. Those few who did not drown immediately were washed in the Everglades, where their bodies were never found. A few people latched onto floating power poles, the bloated carcasses of cows and horses and pieces of attic ceiling that had been blown off the roofs of houses.

Rescuers assigned the morbid task of retrieving the corpses buried the Black bodies where they lay but put the white bodies in trucks and transported them to higher ground. After several days, the workers were unable to keep up with the hundreds of bodies that continued to float out of the back canals and swamps. The bodies were decomposing so quickly that the health department ordered them to be burned. Weeks later, bodies continued turning up in the swamp. Cars and railroad cars delivered 1,600 of them to Port Mayaca, where they were taken to Woodlawn Cemetery and interred in a mass grave.

Other parts of the state also sustained loss of life and property damage. Strong winds and water practically destroyed the Florida East Coast Railway Station in Hallandale. Windows and roofs were damaged in Hollywood and Fort Lauderdale, and power lines and telephone wires were blown down, but the overall damage was comparatively minor. Approximately

This is the mass burial site in West Palm Beach is for African American victims of the 1928 Okeechobee Hurricane. *Wikimedia Commons.*

600 homes were destroyed, and 1,500 others were damaged. City hall was heavily damaged. In West Palm Beach, a pharmacy, warehouse, furniture store, school, ironworks and hotels were completely destroyed. Considerable damage was done to all of the city's theaters. Many of the homes in the African American section of the city suffered major damage as well. In Palm Beach, 1,400 rooms at the Royal Poinciana Hotel were damaged. Approximately 60 percent of the roofs of the Breakers were blown away. The storm washed out roads leading to the bridges at Southern Boulevard and Okeechobee Boulevard. In Jupiter, 50 houses were a total loss; 425 other homes were damaged. The winds were so strong that the Jupiter Inlet Lighthouse swayed about 17 inches and toppled 17 windmills at the Pennock Plantation. Fort Meyers suffered slight property damage. In Central and North Florida, most of the losses were agricultural in nature. Two hundred telephone poles were knocked over in Lake Wales. The inclement weather forced the closure of most of the cigar factories in Tampa.

The total body count was changed several times. In 2003, the number of fatalities was listed as "at least" 2,500, making it one of the worst hurricanes in U.S. history in terms of deaths, second only to the Galveston Hurricane of 1900. Approximately 75 percent of the victims were Black. In addition to the human death toll, 1,278 livestock and 47,389 poultry died in the storm. Throughout the state, 400 telephone poles were broken and 2,500 were leaning, leaving 32,000 households with no phone service. Property damage was estimated at $25 million.

LABOR DAY HURRICANE (1935)

On August 31, 1935, a weather advisor was issued by the National Weather Service stating that a small tropical system was active about 60 miles east of the Bahamas. The storm became a full-fledged hurricane the next day as it passed over the Bahamas. On Labor Day at 8:00 p.m., the storm made landfall around Long Key between Miami and Key West with 185-mile-per-hour winds. After lashing the Keys, the hurricane zigzagged across the southern tip of Florida and carved a 40-mile path of destruction through Tampa, St. Petersburg, Boca Grande, Bradenton and a number of other communities between Key Largo and Marathon. The hurricane headed toward the Gulf of Mexico on September 3, passing above the west coast of Florida. On September 4, the storm struck Cedar Key as a Category 2 hurricane and then blew over Georgia and the Carolinas before moving into the Atlantic Ocean off the coast of Florida and dissipating.

The Labor Day Hurricane of 1935 was the first Category 5 hurricane to strike the United States and is the third-strongest Atlantic hurricane ever recorded. The devastation wrought by the hurricane was horrendous. At least 485 people lost their lives in the storm, 260 of whom were World War I veterans who were hired as work crews in a federal relief project on a portion of the Florida East Coast Railway. The ten-car rescue train sent down from Homestead was swept off the tracks. The accident occurred because the engineer had decided to save time by backing down the single-track line in the hope of reaching the veterans before the storm did. Afterward, searchers discovered bodies at locations miles away, including Cape Sable and Flamingo on the southwest tip of Florida. In an article published in the September 17, 1935 issue of *New Masses* magazine, writer Ernest Hemingway held the government responsible for the tragedy. An investigation conducted by the federal government placed the blame on the whims of nature instead of the mishandling of the evacuation and the Weather Bureau whose first forecast had incorrectly predicted that the hurricane would move through the Florida Straits.

This is a photograph of the mass burial site in Miami's Woodlawn Cemetery of the victims of the Labor Day Hurricane of 1935. *Wikimedia Commons.*

The destructive power of the hurricane was also felt in the village of Islamorada, where almost every building was demolished. Railway embankments and bridges were washed away as well. A sixty- to eighty-mile stretch covering Upper Matecumbe and Lower Matecumbe Keys, Craig Key and Long Key were pummeled by the hurricane. Hundreds of bodies were found along the shores, tangled up in wreckage and mangroves. Corpses that were found three days after the hurricane were placed in wooden boxes.

The impact of the Labor Day Hurricane continued long after it finally disappeared. A number of improvements were made in the way the Weather Bureau tracked hurricanes. Monitory stations were set up all over Florida. After a surge of eighteen to twenty feet above normal washed away the Henry Flagler railroad to Key West, the railroad decided that it would be unwise to try to rebuild during the Great Depression. In 1937, the Florida Division of the Federal Art Project constructed a simple limestone monument on Matecumbe Key, just east of U.S. Route 1 at mile marker 82. A ceramic-tile mural of the Keys in front of the sculpture covers a stone crypt containing the victims' ashes from the makeshift funeral pyres.

MIAMI HURRICANE (1948)

In 1948, six hurricanes and four tropical storms were generated during the hurricane season. Four of the hurricanes were Category 3 or higher. On October 4, Tropical Storm Fox developed in a Category 1 hurricane later in the evening. The National Hurricane Center issued warnings from Fort Myers to Miami. The next day, the warnings were expanded to include Naples to Jupiter. Once the hurricane entered Florida, it moved at a fairly rapid rate.

At noon on October 5, the hurricane was passing over the Keys. The strength of the hurricane subsided for about forty-five minutes between Bahia Honda Bridge and Marathon. By 7:25 p.m., the hurricane had become active again; Bahia Honda Key first felt the impact of the storm's one-hundred-mile-per-hour winds in Florida. The hurricane tore the roofs off several buildings at Naval Air Station Key West over Boca Chica Key. The residents of Biscayne Bay experienced a storm surge of forty-five feet. Miami airport station was inundated with nine and a half inches of rain. The storm also flooded streets in Miami Beach, Miami Springs, Hialeah and Homestead. Near the Miami River, surging waves damaged a Miami bridge. At the Miami International Airport Airport, strong winds flipped

Powerful storm winds generated by the 1948 Miami Hurricane caused damage amounting to thousands of dollars in Key West. *Wikimedia Commons.*

over several planes. Not surprisingly, many homes in Miami experience rampant power outages. In Miami Beach, a fire gutted a meat market.

The hurricane reached the Fort Lauderdale–Pompano area around 9:30 p.m. Three F2 tornadoes were spawned by the storm. One of them demolished three houses at Opa-locka; a second tornado wiped out twenty-five houses at Pompano, resulting in $100,000 worth of property damage, as well as seven injured residents. A third tornado developed forty-five minutes later, setting down in Fort Lauderdale, where it damaged five houses and ripped the roof off a two-story building. Property damage amounted to $15,000. Residents of West Palm Beach experienced wind gusts up to 62 miles per hour. Miraculously, no lives were lost in the hurricane, despite the fact that it had passed over large population centers, like Miami. On the night of October 7, the hurricane's 105-mile-per-hour winds swept down into Bermuda. The hurricane completely dissipated on October 16.

Hurricane Donna

Hurricane Donna, the most powerful hurricane of the 1960 hurricane season, began as a tropical wave near Cape Verde off the African coast on August 29, 1960. The system developed into Tropical Storm Donna on August 30. The storm then started heading across the Atlantic. On September 1, it attained hurricane status. By the time the hurricane passed over the U.S./British Virgin Islands on September 4–5, it was a Category 4 hurricane. When it passed through the southeastern Bahaman Islands and Puerto Rico on September 5, it was still a Category 4 hurricane, drenching Puerto Rico in ten to fifteen inches of rainwater. Floodwaters drowned 107 people in Puerto Rico.

When the hurricane made landfall in the Florida Keys on September 9, it had regained much of the strength it had lost in Puerto Rico, bringing wind gusts up to 138 miles per hour. The storm surge in the Florida Keys was, in some places, thirteen feet above normal. Approximately 75 percent of the buildings in the Keys were heavily damaged. Around 564 homes were completely destroyed. About 1,382 homes were damaged. One person died in the Keys, and seventy-one were injured. A number of subdivisions in Marathon were obliterated. Floodwaters made the Overseas Highway impassable. Between Marathon and Tavernier, approximately 5 percent of the buildings were destroyed. Winds and waves washed away six bridges

Hurricane Donna made landfall in Key West on September 9, 1960. *Wikimedia Commons*.

between Marathon and Craig Key. Docks and boats were severely damaged as well. As the hurricane turned northward, it passed over Naples and Fort Myers, bringing with it surges four to seven feet above normal. In Fort Myers and Daytona Beach, thirteen deaths were reported.

Miami-Dade County also experienced Donna's fury. Floodwaters surged through homes in Homestead and knocked down power lines. In Miami, wind and water uprooted trees, flooded the streets and broke windows, but, for the most part, did minor damage to the buildings. In Dade County, the hurricane destroyed a total of 85 houses and damaged 2,317 houses. Farmers reported extensive crop damage. Boca Raton, Delray Beach and North Palm Beach, on the other hand, emerged from the hurricane relatively unscathed.

Donna inflicted considerable harm on Everglades National Park. Approximately 50 percent of the Everglades' large stands of mangrove trees were completely wiped out by the storm. Almost all of the mangrove trees that had survived the 1935 Labor Day hurricane did not survive the 1960 hurricane. The bird population in the park was also adversely

Boatyards in the Florida Keys sustained heavy damage from Hurricane Donna. *Wikimedia Commons.*

affected by the hurricane. Between 35 and 40 percent of the endangered white herons in the Everglades died in the storm, which also destroyed all of the park's eagle nests. To the relief of park officials, twelve of them were rebuilt within four months.

On September 12, the hurricane slipped back into the Atlantic Ocean. The storm retained its status as a Category 3 hurricane when it struck North Carolina's Outer Banks. The hurricane then made its way up the coast of New England, lashing Rhode Island and Maine with 130-mile-per-hour winds. On the same day, Donna set down in Long Island, New York. By the time the storm reached Maine, its strength was largely depleted.

Donna left behind a legacy of devastation in Florida. Approximately 50 percent of the grapefruit crop and 10 percent of the tangerine and orange crops were destroyed. The avocado crop was practically a total loss. In the hurricane, 14 people perished; 1,188 were injured. Property losses totaled $350 million in Florida. Hurricane Donna remains the only hurricane to produce hurricane-force winds in Florida, the Mid-Atlantic States and New England. The 1960 hurricane also retained its status in the Atlantic Basin for a record amount of time (nine days).

HURRICANE BETSY

Hurricane Betsy is remembered as one of the costliest hurricanes in terms of property damage and human life in American history. When it was photographed by the TIROS weather satellite on August 23, 1965, it was just a weak tropical depression. By the afternoon of August 29, however, the storm had strengthened into a hurricane 200 miles away from Puerto Rico. It lost strength when it looped northward of Puerto Rico, but on September 2, the storm became, once again, a bona fide hurricane. The storm seemed to be on its way to South Carolina when it shifted course back toward Florida on September 4. While passing over the Bahamas and Nassau, its winds reached speeds up to 147 miles per hour. By September 7, Betsy was moving toward Florida once again, edging along southern Florida. When the storm touched down at Key Largo on September 8, it was a Category 3 hurricane.

As the hurricane passed out of Florida into the Gulf, its direction changed once again. On September 9, Betsy headed toward Louisiana, setting down at Grand Isle late in the evening with wind gusts of over one hundred miles per hour. The storm moved inland toward Lafayette on September 9 as a Category 4 hurricane and traveled northward through central Louisiana

Hurricane Betsy was a Category 3 hurricane when it set down in Key West on September 8, 1965. *Wikimedia Commons.*

along the Mississippi River. Floodwaters surged along the Gulf Coast as far as Mobile, Alabama. Most of the buildings in Grand Isle suffered either major damage or complete destruction. Betsy also sank hundreds of boats and barges, one of which was shipping chlorine when it sank near the campus of the University of Louisiana. Betsy's ten-foot storm surge resulted in the worst flooding that New Orleans had experienced in many years. By September 12, Betsy was moving northward along the Ohio River before finally losing its strength in Ohio on September 13.

Betsy's destructive rage first appeared in Florida in the coastal town of Stuart on September 7 when it was a Category 3 hurricane. Its 60-mile-per-hour gusts ripped up awnings and pushed over trees. When Betsy passed over southern Florida, its 165-mile-per-hour winds toppled utility poles, knocking out electrical power and telephone service for hundreds of homes. Debris hurtling through the air destroyed house trailers and blocked roads, like U.S. Highway 1, which was made impassable by fallen telephone poles. Obstructions such as these cut off access from mainland Florida to the Keys. Strong winds also damaged 25 to 50 percent of Florida's citrus crop.

Betsy's storm surge also accounted for much of the damage in Florida's coastal areas. Shoreline property along Biscayne Bay suffered significant water damage. A strong tide surge inflicted massive damage on the peninsula's southern coast. The highest storm surge was around the coast of Key Largo, with a measurement of 9 feet. Areas south of Clearwater on the western coast caused extensive beach erosion. At the Miami Beach waterfront, a 6.1-foot storm tide was responsible for significant property damage, especially along Biscayne Bay, where powerful waves and wind gusts flooded houses and tore three barges from their moorings. Strong winds blew water into hotels and private residences along the waterfront.

Betsy damaged a large number of ships in Florida as well. In Palm Beach, powerful winds created towering waves that forced a freighter to run aground. At Lake Worth inlet, the storm surge caused a second cargo ship, the *Panamanian*, to run aground. The force of the winds blew a fifty-foot sailboat completely out of the water into a neighborhood at Key Largo.

Heavy rainfall was a mixed blessing in South Florida. Plantation Key was drenched with 11.8 inches of rain. Communities as far north as Tampa Bay also experienced heavy rainfall. Ironically, no water damage was reported in these cities and towns. In fact, Betsy brought much-needed rain to the Everglades, which was suffering from the effects of a drought. Betsy also generated two tornadoes in Florida, one near Marathon and one near Big Pine Key. Neither of these cities reported much damage from the twisters.

However, a waterspout near Fort Walton Beach destroyed a marina, along with twelve boats that were docked there.

Hurricane Betsy is the first tropical storm in the United States to cause more than $1 billion in damage. By the time the hurricane dissipated, the final damage figure had reached $1.42 billion. Eighty-one people died, most of them in Louisiana. The damage inflicted by Hurricane Donna in the Lesser Antilles, the Bahamas, Florida, Louisiana, Mississippi, Arkansas, Tennessee and Missouri can be attributed at least in part to its erratic movements. Florida was one of the states affected most by the hurricane, where the storm surge claimed five lives and caused damage totaling $139 million. The destruction inflicted by Hurricane Donna resulted in the creation of the Army Corps of Engineers' Hurricane Protection Program, which built new levees for New Orleans. Because of the hurricane's devastating effects on life and property, the name Betsy was removed from the list of rotating names for storms and hurricanes.

HURRICANE ANDREW

The storm system that eventually became Hurricane Andrew first appeared as a tropical wave from the west coast of Africa on August 1, 1992. After spawning a tropic depression on August 16, it became Tropical Storm Andrew the next day. Even though the storm had nearly dissipated on August 20, the Hurricane Center kept a close watch on it. On August 21, the slow-moving storm turned west–southeast of Nassau. On August 22, the storm attained hurricane status. In the next seventy-four hours, it intensified to Category 5. During that period, the hurricane set down on Eleuthera Island with 160-mile-per-hour winds. On August 24 at 8:40 UTC, Hurricane Andrew made landfall at Elliott Key with 165-mile-per-hour winds, making it the third-most intense hurricane to strike the United States. The Category 5 hurricane then moved near Homestead. After heading west to the Gulf of Mexico, Andrew shifted direction north toward Central Louisiana on August 26 in a diminished state as a Category 3 hurricane. After Andrew set down in Morgan City, its 115-mile-per-hour winds began to diminish in intensity as it headed north and northeast. Not long after Andrew passed into Mississippi in August, its strength dwindled to that of a tropical depression. Moving northeast, the depression combined with a frontal system before dissipating over the Appalachian Mountains.

Andrew remained the costliest hurricane ever to hit Florida until Hurricane Irma in 2017. Most of the destruction was in South Florida, especially Homestead, where 165-mile-per-hour winds leveled many houses to their foundations. By the time Andrew had finally moved out of Florida, it had caused $27.3 billion in damages, destroying over 63,500 houses and damaging 124,000 houses. The human cost was also considerable. In the hurricane, 65 residents of Florida lost their lives, and 150,000 people were left homeless. Andrew also destroyed or damaged 82,000 businesses. The disruption of the lives of many Floridians by the hurricane was so severe that about 1,000 residents of the state moved away, never to come back.

Hurricane Andrew also had a massive environmental impact in Florida. As it passed through Biscayne and Everglades National Park, the hurricane seriously damaged seventy thousand acres of mangrove trees, which tend to absorb the force of hurricanes. Mangrove trees are also important to the environment because they build land by trapping sand and silt in their roots. Also, birds in the Everglades use the branches of mangrove trees as nesting areas. The strong winds affected other trees as well, such as hardwoods, 25 percent of which were defoliated and badly damaged. Andrew damaged 25 percent of the royal palms and 33 percent of the pine

Hurricane Andrew damaged or destroyed every building on Homestead Air Force Base. *NARA & DVIDS Public Domain Archives.*

trees in the Everglades. Interestingly enough, Andrew did not affect wildlife, like alligators, very much at all. The marine environment in south Florida was also adversely affected by Hurricane Andrew, which caused severe bottom scouring and beach over-wash. Increased turbidity in the offshore areas lasted as long as thirty days. Massive blooms of phytoplankton aggravated the turbidity. Fish and invertebrates were harmed by the low dissolved-oxygen concentrations. Fuel continued to leak from damaged boats and marina fuel tanks for twenty-seven days after the hurricane. The destruction caused by Hurricane Andrew is still evident in natural settings, like the Everglades, and in the lives of the people who survived it.

HURRICANE IRMA

As far as Hurricanes go, Hurricane Irma had a long life. On August 27, 2017, it emerged as a tropical wave just west of the Cape Verde Islands. By 12:00 UTC on August 30, the storm had become a tropical depression. Six hours later, the National Hurricane Center categorized it as a tropical depression. On September 4, Irma was gaining strength as it headed toward the northern Leeward Islands. By the next day, it had reached its maximum strength at 6:00 UTC when it was spotted seventy miles east-southeast of Bermuda. The storm was a Category 5 hurricane when it set down on Bermuda on September 5. Irma landed on St. Martin at 11:15 UTC later in the day. At 16:30 UTC on September 6, Irma made landfall on the island of Virgin Gorda in the British Virgin Islands. Between September 6 and September 7, Irma moved toward the northern shore of Puerto Rico and the Dominican Republic. On September 8, Irma set down on Little Inagua Island in the Bahamas at 5:00 UTC. With renewed strength, Irma made landfall near Cayo Romano, Cuba, the morning of September 9. After weakening to Category 4 status, the storm set down in the Cuban Keys.

In the early morning hours of September 10, Irma passed over the Florida Straits. Irma had become a Category 4 hurricane at 6:00 UTC when it was fifty-five miles south–southeast of Key West, Florida. After turning north–northeast, Irma, now a Category 4 hurricane, set down near Cudjo Key in the Florida Keys at 13:00 UTC on September 10. When Irma made landfall near Marco Island, Florida, at 19:30 UTC on September 10, it was a Category 3 hurricane. Irma's intensity weakened as it moved over southwestern Florida. Irma had diminished to Category 2 status when it passed east of Naples

Main Street Road Town in Tortola was severely damaged when Hurricane Irma made landfall in the British Virgin Islands. *Wikimedia Commons.*

and Fort Myers in the early morning hours of September 11. As it passed between Naples and Florida, Irma was a Category 1 storm. By 12:00 UTC on September 11, Irma had become a tropical storm when it was twenty miles west of Gainesville, Florida, and southeastern Georgia. After moving over southern Georgia west of Valdosta at 18:00 UTC on September 11, Irma was a remnant. What remained of Irma crossed into Alabama. On September 13, Irma dissipated over southeastern Missouri.

Hurricane Irma was responsible for ten deaths: seven in Florida, two in Georgia, and one in South Carolina. Of the seven deaths in Florida, three adult males drowned in the lower Florida Keys; two of them were found near their houseboats. In Duval County, an older man and woman drowned when their tent was flooded in the woods. In Manatee County, an eighty-nine-year-old male fell into a canal and drowned as he was attempting to tie up his boat. In Broward County, strong gusts knocked down an eighty-six-year-old male when he opened the front door of his house. He was killed in the fall. The deaths of eighty other people were indirectly caused by the hurricane, such as carbon monoxide poisoning from generators, vehicle accidents and chainsaw accidents.

The most severe hurricane damage in Florida occurred in the Florida Keys, where Irma passed through as a Category 4 hurricane. Approximately 90 percent of the homes in the Middle and Lower Keys were either damaged or destroyed. About 25 percent of the buildings were destroyed, and 65 percent of them were heavily damaged. In addition, forty people were injured. More people would have been killed or injured had not 75 percent of the residents in the Keys evacuated ahead of the hurricane.

Communities on mainland Florida were also severely affected by Irma. In Collier County, Irma was a Category 3 hurricane when it destroyed 88 buildings and damaged 1,500. Powerful winds knocked down trees and utility poles in Golden Gate, Marco Island and Naples. Approximately 1,000 homes were severely damaged in Miami-Dade County. The agricultural industry suffered $245 million in losses. Although Hurricane Irma gradually lost strength as it moved through Florida, it caused significant damage to many buildings, trees and power poles. Over 7,000 homes in Brevard were damaged, and 450 homes were destroyed. In Osceola County near Orland, 4,000 buildings were damaged. Property damage was near $100 million. Losses from damage to orange groves in southwest and central Florida totaled $100 million. For the most part, property damage in northern Florida resulted from flooding. The floodwaters that Irma brought to Jacksonville were the highest in the city's history. Some homes and businesses in the northeastern portion of Florida were damaged by wind gusts and tornadoes.

Hurricane Irma will be remembered as the first Category 5 hurricane to hit the Leeward Islands. At the time, Irma was the most powerful hurricane to pass through the open Atlantic, outside of the Caribbean Sea and the Gulf of Mexico. Finally, Hurricane Irma is the third-strongest Atlantic hurricane to make landfall ever recorded.

HURRICANE IAN

Hurricane Ian first manifested as a tropical wave off the west coast of Africa on September 14, 2022. The atmospheric disturbance weakened as it traveled south toward the Cape Verde Islands on September 18. Over the next twenty-four hours, it tracked toward the Windward Islands. On September 21, the wave made its way to the southeast Caribbean, not far from the ABC Islands. By the morning of September 23, the National Hurricane Center had designated the storm Tropical Depression Nine. Later that afternoon, the depression acquired the designation Tropical Storm Ian. At 8:30 UTC, Ian struck Pinar del Rio Province in Cuba. The storm intensified as it left Cuba and entered the Gulf of Mexico. Ian grew stronger in the Dry Tortugas and became a Category 4 hurricane on September 28 at 9:00 UTC. At 10:35,

Ian approached Southwest Florida with wind gusts of twenty-six miles per hour. At 9:05 UTC, Ian made landfall at Cayo Costa. About ninety minutes later, the hurricane set down near Pirate Harbor. Toward the end of the day, Ian weakened to tropical storm status as it moved to the eastern Florida coastline. On September, Ian sped toward the South Carolina coast. Ian made landfall at Georgetown, South Carolina, at 18:00 UTC. Three hours later, Ian weakened to a post tropical cycle as it reached the South Carolina Coast. The cyclone completely dissipated at 3:00 UTC on October 2.

Hurricane Ian's impact began even before it made landfall on September 28. On September 27, eleven of the twelve tornadoes spawned by Hurricane Ian touched down in the Miami metropolitan area. One of them heavily damaged twenty aircraft and a number of hangers at the North Perry Airport. Later that night, a tornado wrecked several cars and blew the roofs of a number of houses in Kings Point in Palm Beach County. It also blew down a tree on top of an apartment building. A third tornado uprooted a large number of trees in Wellington and Loxahatchee.

Southwest Florida first experienced the fury of Hurricane Ian in the form of ten- to fifteen-foot storm surge. Residents of Naples were trapped in homes and parking garages by rising floodwaters. A fire station in Naples was also flooded. Ian caused $2.2 billion in property damage in Collier County and $948 million in unincorporated areas.

The Florida Keys were also heavily affected by strong wind gusts and storm surges. Flooding along the coast of Key West inundated 93 homes, 38 of which were severely damaged. The surge also destroyed 14 homes and 14 businesses in Key West. In Big Pine Key, approximately ten thousand electrical subscribers lost power. Around 150 vessels were torn loose from the dock throughout the Florida Keys.

Floodwaters also surged through Naples, trapping people in their cars and houses. The first floor of several parking garages and a fire station were completely flooded. In North Naples, the flooding of an ambulance bay and a helipad impeded efforts to transport people to the hospital. Property damages in Naples totaled $989 million and $256 million in Marco Island.

Lee County was hit particularly hard by Hurricane Ian. Approximately 52,514 homes and other buildings were damaged, Approximately 5,369 buildings were completely destroyed. Building damages amounted to $6.8 billion. Ian also washed away a large part of the Sanibel Causeway. The Matlacha Bridge, which was Pine Island's access to the mainland, was also destroyed. Trees, road signs, traffic lights and electrical poles in the area collapsed, cutting off electrical services and communication.

In the aftermath of Hurricane Ian, many streets and roads became impassable in North Port. *Wikimedia Commons*.

The storm surge also accounted for much of the heavy damage in the southwest tip of Florida. Because of the damage to 525 buildings and homes in Lee County, property damages totaled $6.8 billon. Strong winds blew down utility poles and trees. Damages in Hendry County totaled $419,000, primarily because of hurricane-force wind gusts. In Charlotte County, around 200 homes were demolished. In Mantee County, Ian destroyed 10 buildings and heavily damaged 296 structures. Damages in Mantee County totaled $1.1 billion. Wauchuca in Hardee County experienced major damage to 114 buildings and homes.

In Central Florida, powerful winds were responsible for $1.4 million in minor damage to 113 buildings. On Fort Pierce Beach, wind gusts blew hundreds of sea turtle eggs out of their nests in the sand, damaging hundreds of them. Approximately 900 businesses and 3,200 homes suffered water damage from floodwaters. In Osceola County, floodwaters caused the worst damage in the county to St. Cloud and Kissimmee.

High water levels produced severe flooding in most of Orlando's neighborhoods, necessitating the rescue of around 250 people. Orange County reported property damage of $206 million. In Lake County, flooding from St. John's River did minor damage to 61 structures and major damage to 41. Astor suffered damage to 49 structures and major damage to 49 others. Damage estimates totaled $4.5 million. Seawalls near Daytona Beach were damaged by massive storm surges. Floodwaters produced by 21 inches of rain in New Smyrna Beach were so high that 180 people had to be evacuated. Even though the Kennedy Space Center was pummeled by 108-mile-per-hour wind gusts, only minor damage was reported.

Although Ian skirted Tampa Bay, nearby counties did feel the destructive power of strong winds. In Hillsborough County, wind gusts between sixty-five and seventy-five miles per hour caused $54.8 million in property damage. One-third of the customers in Pinellas County lost power. Approximately $22.6 million in property damage was reported in the county.

Ian raged through parts of the First Coast with heavy downpours and strong winds. The Flagler Beach Pier was damaged by strong wind gusts in Flagler. Homes and roads were also inundated in Flagler County. Floodwaters washed over roads in St. Augustine and forced residents out of their homes on Anastasia Island. Trees that were blown down at Naval Air Station Jacksonville damaged several homes. In Nassau County, the Fernandina Beach marina and Fernandina High School were nearly destroyed by the storm surge.

Hurricane Ian will be remembered as the most destructive cyclone since the 1935 Labor Day Hurricane. Property losses amounted to more than $50 billion, mostly as the result of flooding. Ian caused 157 deaths in total, 146 of which occurred in Florida.

HURRICANE NICOLE

On November 4, 2022, an atmospheric disturbance was detected in the southwestern Atlantic Ocean. The next day, it carried thunderstorms north to Puerto Rico. On November 6, it began to strengthen with wind speeds of forty-five miles per hour. The next day, the National Hurricane Center designated the disturbance as Subtropical Storm Nicole. On November 8, the storm intensified as a tropical cyclone, which set down the next day on Grand Bahama as a Category 1 hurricane. On November 10, Nicole made landfall on Hutchinson Island south of Vero Beach. The hurricane crossed central and northern Florida and southern Georgia. Toward the end of the day, the hurricane moved into the Gulf of Mexico and turned north to Cedar Key, As the hurricane headed toward southwest Georgia, it began to weaken. By November 11, Nicole had become a post-tropical cycle over West Virginia. The former hurricane finally dissipated over the eastern coast.

Nicole's massive storm surge inundated Florida's east coast. Ironically, many of the buildings that Hurricane Ian had damaged were completely destroyed by the erosion Nicole's rains created on the beach. Erosion also washed out a section of roadway in Vero Beach and unearthed the remains of Native Americans on South Hutchinson Island.

The residents of Florida were directly affected by Hurricane Nicole. Five people died in the hurricane. Two of them were killed in an automobile accident. Two more were electrocuted by downed power lines. Searchers discovered one more body on a yacht. Over 300,000 customers lost power across the state of Florida, thanks to Hurricane Nicole.

FLORIDA WILDFIRES (1998)

Northeast Florida

In the minds of most people, Florida's high humidity and excessive rainfall have made it immune to wildfire. The above-average rainfall produced by an El Niño in the winter of 1998 nurtured an abundance of vegetation and undergrowth in the woodland areas. When the rainfall abruptly ceased between May and July 1998, the drought index rose to 700 (out of 800), creating ideal conditions for wildfires. The fire risk was intensified by the increased development in rural areas, with plants and trees growing near houses without municipal water systems and fire hydrants. Record high temperatures in the summer only exacerbated the problem.

In mid-May 1998, dry thunderstorms were producing thunder and lightning every day; however, most of the rain evaporated before striking the ground. Lightning was responsible for most of the fires, the largest of which broke out in Brevard, Osceola, Orange, Seminole, St. John's, Flagler, Duval and Volusia Counties. In the first week of June, the brush fires were headed toward Jacksonville and St. Augustine, putting thousands of lives in danger. On June 15, Governor Lawton Chiles declared a state of emergency. I-95 was closed down because of fires burning in the area. By late June, around eighty fires were being reported daily. Fire or emergency status was reported in all sixty-seven Florida counties. The largest concentration of fires flamed up in north and central Florida. Helicopters and fixed-wing aircraft were called in to assist firefighters. By July 1, the wildfires had jumped I-95. On July 4, outbreaks forced the closure of I-95 from Jacksonville to Titusville. Government officials were concerned that these small fires would eventually merge into massive fires. By this time, strong westerly winds were driving the wildfires to the heavily populated areas along the coast, threatening communities between Flagler and Brevard, a total of 500,000 residents. The wildfires also posed a threat to the 200,000 visitors who were expected to attend the NASCAR event at the Daytona International Speedway. The race was canceled on July 2. Later in July, Governor Chiles ordered the evacuation of Flagler County's 45,000 residents, the first and last time in Florida's history that wildfires forced such a mass evacuation. Local firefighters on the Palm Coast, who were battling hundreds of fires, were aided by hundreds of first-response crews from Florida and the rest of the nation, including California. In one of the few humorous footnotes to the conflagration, a call for bandanas prompted people across America to send thousands of bananas instead.

This firefighter is one of many who fought the four-day Panorama brush fire, which spread from canyons north of town. *NARA 7 DVIDS Public Domain Archives.*

On July 5, the firefighters breathed a sigh of relief as rain clouds began to form. By mid-July, most of the wildfires were under control. After all the fires had finally been extinguished, 150 homes and buildings were destroyed. In addition, more than $300 million of timber had been incinerated. On July 4, the *New York Times* reported that the total cost of fighting the fires had amounted to $80 million. The wildfires were not directly responsible for any deaths, but the crew of a Sikorsky Skycrane lost their lives because of a mechanical failure. Aside from the loss of property, the citizens of Florida suffered other ill effects of the wildfires, including burns, injuries, heat-related illnesses, injuries, mental health issues, traffic accidents and respiratory problems. Many evacuees were unable to return to their homes for days. One victim of the wildfires, Coleen Harris, recalled the fateful day when she witnessed the wildfires encroaching on her home: "I went to the front door and saw the fire was real, real close. In ten minutes, we had the horse loaded up, got the kids and the dogs and got the heck out of there." Stories like hers were repeated thousands of time during the 199 wildfires. As a result of the catastrophe, the Palm Coast Fire Department expanded with five fire stations, fifty-seven career firefighters, and over fifty volunteer firefighters and fire police.

THE GROUNDHOG DAY TORNADO OUTBREAK

Central Florida

On the morning of February 2, 2007, abnormally high temperatures, together with a powerful jet stream and increased moisture, produced strong vertical wind shear from the ground up, causing thunderstorms to rotate and develop into tornadoes. Within sixty-seven minutes, three full-strength tornadoes inflicted damage to property and buildings along a seventy-mile track.

The first tornado set down in Sumter County and crossed into Lake County at 3:06 a.m. At the time, many homeowners in the area were sound asleep, despite warnings from the weather service the day before. By the time the tornado had dissipated, it had destroyed 200 homes and damaged 3,134 others in Sumter County. Its powerful winds flew down the walls of houses, uprooted trees and obliterated mobile homes. The tornado also destroyed 101 homes and damaged 180 others in Lake County. A total of seventy-six people were injured, and twenty-one people were killed.

This church in Lady Lake was flattened by one of the three tornadoes that made landfall in Central Florida on Groundhog Day, 2007. *NARA 7DVIDS Public Domain Archives.*

At 3:37 a.m., the second tornado touched ground in the Lake Mack area, killing thirteen people and damaging or destroying 500 homes and other structures, including WCFB FM's 1,500-foot-high radio tower.

At 4:22 a.m., the third tornado took shape in Volusia County. It stayed on the ground for three minutes until it passed thought the intracoastal waterway in New Smyrna Beach. The tornado's three-mile path of devastation was lined with damaged carports, roofs and garage doors. No one died in the third tornado, but twenty-five houses were completely destroyed.

The Ground Hog Day outbreak of tornadoes was the second deadliest in Florida's history. Property loss totaled $218 million. To prevent the loss of life on this scale, Weather Emergency Alerts were created.

6

PLANE CRASHES IN THE EVERGLADES

Eastern Flight 401 (1972)

The crash of Eastern Air Lines 401 is one of the most analyzed aviation catastrophes in history. In the early 1970s, the Lockheed L-1011-1 Tristar, the first airliner that Eastern Air Lines had acquired during the spring of 1972, was beset with technical problems. However, the L-1011 that was flying on Flight 401, Flight 310, had fewer "bugs" than most of the other airliners. One of the inaugural L-1011 routes, Flight 401 carried "snowbirds" seeking warmer climes from New York's Kennedy International Airport to Miami International Airport. The pilot was Captain Robert "Bob" Loft. The fifty-five-year-old captain had thirty-two years' experience flying for Eastern. Also in the cockpit on that flight were First Officer Albert Stockstill, Flight Engineer Donald Repo, Maintenance Specialist Angelo Donadeo and an off-duty pilot. Although Loft had nearly thirty thousand flying hours, neither he nor the other men in the cockpit had logged much time on the new L-1011s. Flight 401 flew out of JFK Airport at 9:20 p.m. on December 29, 1972.

Before the crash, Flight 401 was fairly routine, with a few highlights. Edward Ulrich (forty-four) proposed to his girlfriend, Sandra Burt (thirty-two). Stewardess Mercedes Ruiz took a group photograph of the other

A Lockheed L-1011-1 Tristar, similar to this plane flying for All Nippon Airways, crashed in the Everglades on December 29, 1972. *Wikimedia Archives.*

flight attendants because they would be transferred to different planes at the end of the month. Sadly, two of the stewardesses in the photograph—Pat Ghyssels and Stephanie Stanich—did not survive the crash. A passenger, Jerry Eskow, wrote a note on the back of an envelope to Samuel L. Higginbottom, the president and COO of Eastern Airlines: "The ride is smooth, the service is excellent, the plane is beautiful, the pilots are terrific, and I want to particularly compliment your stewardess Jennifer Larson." He put the envelope in his pocket and fell asleep.

At 11:32 p.m., Flight 401 initiated contact with the air traffic controller in Miami. As the plane crossed the Palmetto Expressway just west of the airport, Donadeo noticed that the light indicating that the nose landing gear was down was unlit. Loft requested permission from the tower to enter a holding pattern over the Everglades instead of continuing their approach to the Miami Airport. Stockstill and Repo climbed down the trapdoor on the floor of the cockpit. While the men were in the "hellhole," they tried to remove the light assembly and examine the bulb, but it jammed. At 11:38, Loft informed the tower that he and the crew were going to head west a little farther to see if they could get the light to come on. At this time, the plane was at half its assigned altitude.

As the plane started to turn, 18.7 miles from the end of the runway, it was traveling 227 miles per hour. Suddenly, the left wingtip hit the ground, followed by the left engine and the left landing gear. Then the main part of the fuselage began plowing through the grass and water, scattering metal fragments, passenger seats and cabin fittings over a wide area over the swampy terrain. It skidded through the muck for about a third of a mile. When the starboard wing was ripped off the fuselage, it gouged a fifty-nine-foot-long crater in the mushy ground.

First on the scene were Robert "Bub" Marquis and Ray Dickinson. They had been riding through the swamp in their airboat, catching frogs. People were lying in the wreckage of the plane, screaming and crying. Some of them had their clothes ripped off in the crash. Jet fuel was burning on land and water. The two frog hunters jumped into the water and began saving people. Their primary concern was the passengers who were sitting upside down in their seats in the water. A short while later, a Coast Guard helicopter arrived, landing on a flood-control levee. Rescuers leaped from the helicopter and assisted Marquis and Dickinson with the rescue operation. The frog hunters ferried survivors over to the levee in their airboat. After a short while, the men located the cockpit. Captain Loft was alive but barely. He died a few minutes after being found. First Officer Stockstill lay next to Captain Loft, dead. Flight Engineer Don Repo and Angelo Donadeo were alive.

After fifty-four minutes, the first passengers were airlifted from the crash site. Initially, 79 people and a dog survived. However, 2 of the survivors died at Mercy Hospital in Hialeah, including Don Repo. Of the 176 people on board, 75 survived and 101 died, the largest death toll in the United States involving one airplane at the time. Investigators determined that the soft surface accounted for the high survival rate. They also found that the landing gear was down and locked the entire time, but the flight crew was unaware of it because the nose gear light had burned out. The Transportation Safety Board (NTSB) blamed the crash on the crew, who had failed to monitor the instruments during the final four minutes of flight. Distracted by the problem with the nose gear light, the crew paid no attention to the altitude alert. The crew was unaware that the plane was descending because of the absence of lights in the swamp. As a result of the crash, a number of airlines initiated crew resource management training for their pilots. In addition, flashlights became standard equipment on all aircraft.

The legacy of Flight 401 did not end with improved flight requirements. In 1976, John G. Fuller's book *The Ghost of Flight 401* was published. Fuller's book includes reports of the sudden appearances of the ghosts of Loft and Repo on other Eastern Air Lines flights. The first sighting occurred when one of Eastern Air Lines' L-1011s was on a flight to Mexico. A flight attendant was walking through the galley when she saw the face of a man in the window of one of the ovens. She got the attention of another stewardess, who confirmed that the image of a man's face was indeed on the oven window. The pair brought the flight engineer over to the galley. He recognized the face as being that of Don Repo. The face then began speaking. It told the crew members to watch out for fire on the plane. When the plane landed, an inspection of the plane found that one of the three engines was in need of repair. The crew decided to remove all of the passengers and fly the empty plane back home. Soon after the plane took off, two of the engines flamed out, forcing the pilot to make an emergency landing. Afterward, the crew admitted that the ghost of Don Repo had helped them through the landing.

After this incident, a number of sightings of the ghosts of Don Repo and Bob Loft were reported from other aircraft. Repo's ghost appeared more often than Loft's ghost. Fuller explained the sightings by the Eastern Air Lines' decision to reuse parts of the L-100 that crashed in the Everglades on Flight 401. Fuller insisted that Eastern Air Lines had tried to cover up this fact. The story goes that even though Eastern Air Lines denied that its planes were haunted, all of the parts salvaged from Aircraft 310 were replaced. A made-for-television movie, *The Ghost of Flight 401*, aired on NBC in February 1978. The CEO of Eastern Air Lines, Frank Borman, called the book and movie "garbage." He considered suing in 1980 for libel but decided that a lawsuit would only give the book and movie more publicity. In the 1980 book *From the Captain to the Colonel: An Informal History of Eastern Airlines*, author Robert J. Serling asserted that the claims that Eastern reused parts from Flight 401 were false.

ValuJet Airlines Flight 592 (1996)

As of this writing, the crash of Flight 592 is the deadliest plane crash in Florida history. On May 11, 1996, Value Airlines' Flight 592 took off from Miami International Airport. The McDonnell Douglas DC-9 was en route to Hartsfield-Jackson Atlanta International Airport. Ten minutes after takeoff, the pilot reported smoke in the cockpit. At the same time, the pilots, Captain Candi Kubeck (thirty-five) and First Officer Richard Hazen (fifty-two), heard a loud bang in their headsets; they really became alarmed when the plane began losing power. Shouts of "Fire! Fire! Fire!" from the passengers were clearly audible in the cockpit voice recorder. A few seconds later, the plane plummeted into a deep-water swamp with a limestone floor in the Everglades.

The exact time of impact was 2:12:42 p.m. Only fragments of the plane were found, and 5 crew members and 105 passengers perished in the crash. Recovery of the bodies was impeded by alligators and sawgrass. The risk of bacterial infection was constantly on the minds of the searchers. Once ValuJet received word of the crash, Luis Laughlin, vice president of people and customer relations, chartered several buses to transport the victims' family members to the crash site to retrieve any of their possessions lying on the ground or floating in the water. Recovery of the victims themselves required several weeks. Approximately 68 of the 110 occupants of the plane could be identified from jawbones, teeth and pieces of flesh. Captain Kubeck's remains were never found. Kubeck's husband was visibly shaken when he picked up his wife's car keys from the muck.

Afterward, investigators determined that the cause of the crash was a fire that burned from the cargo hold throughout the cockpit. Later, investigators

A McDonnell Douglas DC-9 crashed in the Everglades on May 11, 1996. *Wikimedia Commons.*

learned from an outside company's employees that chemical oxygen generators that had been removed from a newly acquired used aircraft were loaded onto Flight 592. Because the chemical oxygen generators had exceeded their expiration date, they were assumed to be empty. Investigators concluded that the canisters must have activated soon after takeoff and sparked the terrible fire.

ValuJet was well known for its poor safety record long before the crash. Its safety record was so bad, in fact, that in 1995, the U.S. military rejected ValueJet's bid to fly military personnel. On June 16, 1996, the FAS grounded ValuJet. On September 30, the airline was allowed to schedule flights again, even though ValuJet's accident rate was fourteen times higher than that of the other airlines. The negative publicity took a heavy toll on the airline. ValuJet acquired AirTran Airways and began operating under AirTran's name. In 2011, Southwest Airlines purchased AirTran, virtually eliminating all traces of ValuJet.

7

SERIAL KILLERS

OSCAR RAY BOLIN

Oscar Ray Bolin was born in Portland, Oregon, on January 22, 1962, in a family of carnival workers and manual laborers. He and his family led a nomadic lifestyle through Indiana, Ohio, Kentucky and several other states. His parents abused and humiliated him as he was growing up. Bolin received regular beatings from his father; one day, his mother led him to the bus stop on a leash. Bolin began committing crimes as a teenager. For example, at the age of fifteen, he was arrested in Ohio on the charge of theft. Around 1980, he moved to Florida, where he was employed as a carnival worker. According to Bolin's girlfriend Cheryl Haffner, he abducted her and drove her around Tampa for several hours. At the end of the ride, she reported him to the police, who charged him with false imprisonment. Not long thereafter, the charge was dropped; the next year, Haffner and Bolin were married in Tampa.

Bolin's propensity for kidnapping and murdering young women began on January 25, 1986. A manager at Church's Fried Chicken named Blanche Holley and a co-worker completed their shift at the store and closed up. She left the building at 1:30 a.m. and walked toward her car. A few hours later, a jogger discovered the young woman's body in an orange grove. Investigators determined that she had been stabbed to death.

Seventeen-year-old Stephanie Collins became Bolin's second victim on November 15, 1986. The Chamberlain High School student had finished her shift at the drugstore where she worked part-time and walked toward her car in the parking lot. This was the last time anyone ever saw her alive. On December 5, 1986, her corpse was discovered wrapped up in sheets and towels. Not only did her body exhibit several stab wounds, but her skull was crushed as well.

On December 5, 1986, twenty-six-year-old Teri Lynn Matthews drove to the post office to pick up the family's mail on her way home from work at 2:48 p.m., according to security camera footage. Police suspected that foul play had taken place when they found her car parked outside of the post office with the engine running. Her body, wrapped in a white sheet, was discovered in a patch of woods a few hours later. She had been stabbed multiple times, and her throat was cut.

The murders of Holley, Collins and Matthews remained unsolved until 1990 when Bolin's ex-wife, Cheryl Coby, informed police through her current husband that Bolin had told her that he had killed Matthews and that his thirteen-year-old half brother, Phillip, had helped him disposed of the body. After Phillip admitted to helping Bolin bury the body, the authorities charged Bolin with Matthews's murder. At the time, Bolin was serving a twenty-five to seventy-five-year sentence for kidnapping and raping a twenty-year-old waitress in Toledo, Ohio, in 1987. He released her after the gun he had intended to shoot her with jammed.

In July 1991, Bolin was charged with the murder of all three women and sentenced to death for each of them. On January 7, 2016, Bolin was executed by lethal injection after being incarcerated for twenty-eight years.

TED BUNDY

Ted Bundy clearly did not fit the profile of the typical serial killer. He was born on November 24, 1946, in Burlington, Vermont, to an unwed mother named Eleanor Louise Cowell. The identity of his biological father has never been determined. He was raised as his grandparents' adopted son to conceal his illegitimate birth. Ted's mother married Johnnie Bundy in 1951 and soon started a family with him. In addition to raising her children, Eleanor worked as a secretary. Growing up, Ted proved to be a good student who did not interact much with kids his own age. Ted went on to earn a degree in psychology from the University of Washington in 1972. While he was there, Ted dated a pretty, dark-haired girl. After they broke up, most of the girls he dated in the years to follow resembled his first true love.

No one knows for certain when Ted's murderous rampage began, although most authorities agree that he probably started killing women in Oregon in 1974. Because of his handsome appearance, many women dropped their guard in his presence. As a rule, he preyed on the kindness of women whom he tricked into climbing into his car by pretending to be injured. He usually raped his "Good Samaritans" before beating them to death. Bundy's killing spree is believed to have extended through several states.

Bundy's assaults against women first came to the attention of investigators in the mid- to late 1970s when he was enrolled in law school. In 1975, police searched his car and discovered a cache of burglary tools, like a rope, a mask and handcuffs. In 1977, Bundy received a one- to five-year jail sentence after a young lady he had kidnapped, Carol DaRonch, escaped and alerted the police. In 1977, Bundy was incarcerated after kidnapping a Colorado woman; he escaped by jumping out of the library window. Bundy was apprehended and returned to jail eight days later. In November of that year, Bundy broke out of jail by climbing through a hole he had made in the ceiling of his jail cell.

Bundy was able to flee to Tallahassee because his absence was not detected until fifteen hours after his escape. At 3:00 a.m. on January 14, 1978, Bundy forced his way into Florida State University's Chi Omega sorority house. Using a piece of firewood, he bludgeoned Margaret Bowman and Lisa Levy and then strangled them to death with stockings. He also attacked Kathy Kleiner and Karen Chandler, but they survived their injuries. Under the cover of darkness, he walked several blocks and broke into an apartment rented by another girl, Cheryl Thomas. He beat her so severely that she lost her sense of hearing, but she survived.

Bundy's criminal career came to an abrupt end in 1978. On February 9, he kidnapped and murdered a twelve-year-old girl in Lake City Junior High School in Lake City, Florida. He hid Kimberly Leach's body in Sewanee River State Park under a shed. On February 15, 1978, Pensacola policeman David Lee pulled Bundy over at 1:30 a.m. for driving with his headlights off. Bundy violently resisted arrest until Lee finally subdued him. At first, Bundy refused to tell the policeman his real name, but after a few minutes, he finally admitted that he was on the FBI's most-wanted list.

Bundy was indicted for murder on July 18, 1979. Eleven days later, the jury found him guilty of the first-degree murders of Levy and Bowman.

Ted Bundy's 1968 Volkswagen Beetle and John Dillinger's 1834 Essex Terraplane 8 getaway car are on display at Alcatraz East Crime Museum in Pigeon Forge, Tennessee. *Wikimedia Commons.*

He was also convicted of the attempted murder of Chandler, Thomas and Kleiner. The next week, the judge sentenced him to death in the electric chair. On January 7, 1980, Bundy went on trial in Orlando for the murder of a twelve-year-old girl. During the trial, a firefighter testified that he saw Bundy escort the child into his van. Clothing fibers matching Bundy to the victim sealed his fate. Once again, a jury found him guilty of murder. On July 4, 1979, Bundy was sentenced to death.

Bundy's execution was scheduled for January 25, 1989. As he was being strapped into the electric chair, "Old Sparky," a mob of over two hundred people were standing outside of the prison doors. When Superintendent Tom Barton asked him if he had any last words, Bundy said, "I'd like to give my love to my family and friends." After his mouth and chin were covered with a thick strap, a metal skullcap was placed on his head. Barton then signaled to the anonymous executioner, who pushed the button. Instantly, two thousand volts of electricity coursed through his body. Bundy's body stiffened for a few seconds before going limp. A wisp of smoke rose from his right leg. At 7:16 a.m., the doctor pronounced Ted Bundy dead. In accordance with his wishes, his body was cremated, and his ashes were scattered over Washington's Cascade Mountains.

Over the years, Ted Bundy has captured the imagination of filmmakers and authors alike. Movies about Ted Bundy include *The Deliberate Stranger* (1986), *The Stranger Beside Me* (2003), *The Riverman* (2004), *Bundy: An American Icon* (2008), *The Capture of the Green River Killer* (2008), *Extremely Wicked, Shockingly Evil and Vile* (2019), *American Boogeyman* (2021), *Ted Bundy* (2021) and *No Man of God* (2021). Several television documentaries about Bundy have also been produced, including *Ted Bundy: Devil in Disguise*, *Ted Bundy: An American Monster*, *Ted Bundy: What Happened*, *Conversations with a Killer: The Ted Bundy Tapes* and *Ted Bundy: Falling for a Killer*. Books include Ann Rule's *The Stranger Beside Me* (1980), Elizabeth Kendall's *The Phantom Prince: My Life with Ted Bundy* (1981), Kevin Sullivan's *The Bundy Murders: A Comprehensive History* (2009), Michael Stephen's and Hugh Aynesworth's *Ted Bundy: Conversations with a Killer* (2000), Polly Nelson's *Defending the Devil: My Story as Ted Bundy's Last Lawyer* (2019) and Stephen Michaud's and Hugh Aynesworth's *The Only Living Witness: The True Story of Serial Killer Ted Bundy* (2012). Surprisingly, Ted Bundy has also inspired a number of songs, including Jane's Addiction's "Just Admit," Penelope Scott's "True Addiction," Tin Machine's "Video Crimes" and Theory of a Deadman's "Ted Bundy."

David Alan Gore

David Alan Gore was born in Florida on August 21, 1953. Growing up in Indian River County, he became fascinated with firearms, even working as a gunsmith for a while. Unfortunately, he also became enamored of women. In fact, he was fired from his first job as a gas station attendant for boring a peephole between the men's and women's bathrooms. In 1976, Gore paired up with his younger cousin Fred Waterfield to assault several women, all of whom were traveling alone. Their first intended victim was able to run away after Waterfield shot holes in her tires with his rifle outside Yeehaw Junction. They stalked her for a while but gave up after she parked on a busy street. The inept molesters did manage to rape one woman in Vero Beach, but all charges were dropped later because of her reluctance to discuss the assault in a crowded courtroom. As time passed, Gore became an auxiliary sheriff's deputy as well as the caretaker of a citrus grove.

Waterfield, who was employed at an auto shop in Orland, told Gore that the secluded orchard was the ideal spot to lure and rape girls. Gore agreed to take part in the scheme after Waterfield offered him $1,000 for every pretty girl he could bring to the citrus grove.

On February 19, 1981, Gore and Waterfield added murder to their growing list of crimes. Gore was watching high school students disembark from a school bus when he focused his attention on a seventeen-year-old Ying Hua Ling. Flashing his badge, he instructed the frightened girl to climb into his car. He then drove her to her home. When her forty-eight-year-old mother, Hsiang Huang Ling, let them come inside, Gore flashed his badge and then announced that he was arresting the two of them. He then handcuffed them and called up his cousin in Orlando, who told Gore to take the women to the orchard. After Gore drove them to the orchard, he raped them while waiting for his cousin. When Waterfield arrived, the men tied Hsiang Huang Ling to a tree first and then raped her daughter. Unknown to the rapists, Hsiang was slowly choking to death while they raped her daughter. Before leaving the scene of the crime, the men murdered Hsiang, dismembered both of their victims and stuffed their remains in oil drums, which they buried.

On July 15, 1981, the "Killing Cousins," as the men became known, struck again. Gore was driving around Round Island, searching for a blond victim, when he spotted thirty-five-year-old Judith Dailey. Gore disabled her car in a parking lot and "came to her rescue" by offering to drive her to a payphone. Once she was in the pickup truck, Gore handcuffed her at gunpoint and drove to the orchard. On the way, he called Waterfield and told him to meet him at the orchard. After the men raped and murdered Dailey, they dumped her corpse in a swamp ten miles west of Interstate Highway 95. Waterfield paid Gore for procuring another victim with a check for $1,500.

The pair's crime spree came to a temporary hiatus on July 22, 1981. Gore stopped a teenage girl on a country road. Displaying his badge, he told the girl he was going to "hold her for questioning." When her father filed a complaint, Gore was forced to surrender his badge. He was arrested a week later on Vero Beach when officers found him crouched in the back seat of a woman's car with a police radio scanner, a pistol and handcuffs. At the end of the trial, a jury convicted Gore of armed trespassing. Gore received a prison sentence of five years but was paroled in March 1983.

Following Gore's release from prison, he and his cousin resumed their pattern of abducting and killing young women. On May 20, 1983, they picked up two fourteen-year-old hitchhikers—Angelica LaVallee and

Barbara Ann Byer. They drove the girls to the citrus grove, where they raped both girls and shot them. The pair interred Byer's dismembered remains in a shallow grave. LaVallee's corpse was dumped in a nearby canal.

Gore and Waterfield's last victims were Regan Martin (fourteen) and Lynn Elliott (seventeen). They were students at Vero Beach High School. On July 26, 1983, they were hitchhiking to Wabasso Beach when Gore and Waterfield pulled their pickup truck over on the shoulder and offered to drive the girls to the beach. Once the girls were in the truck, the men drove them to a house owned by Gore's relatives. Waterfield lost his nerve after seeing his sister during the drive and took off. Gore ordered the girls to enter the house at gunpoint and placed them in separate rooms. While Gore was raping Martin, Elliott managed to escape to the driveway, despite the fact that she was nude and her hands were tied behind her back. Afterward, Gore confessed to catching up with Elliott after she tripped and fell on the drive and shooting her twice in the head. After killing the girl, Gore, who was also naked, realized that he had been seen by a boy riding a bicycle in the neighborhood. The boy immediately contacted the police. When officers arrived on the scene, they noticed blood dripping from the trunk of a car. Opening the lid, they found Elliott's bloody corpse lying in the fetal position. Gore opened fire on the police, and a fierce gunfight ensued. After ninety minutes, Gore realized that he was hopelessly outgunned and surrendered. He led the police up to the attic, where they found Martin, naked and trussed up with electrical cords.

Gore's subsequent cooperation led to closure for his victims' loved ones. Not only did he show police where he had buried the remains of Barbara Ann Byer, Hsiang Huang Ling and Ying Hua Ling, but he also confessed to the murders of two other women and three girls. On May 17, 1984, the jury convicted Gore of first-degree murder and sentenced him to death. Waterfield was convicted of the murders of LaVallee and Byer on January 21, 1985. He received two death sentences. Gore was executed by lethal injection on April 12, 2012.

BOBBY LONG

Born on October 14, 1953, in Kenova, West Virginia, Bobby Joe Long had a particularly traumatic childhood. As a boy, he frequently slept in the same bed as his mother, Louella, until he was thirteen. Her habit of bringing home men she met at the bar where she worked as a cocktail waitress undoubtedly contributed to his negative views toward women. Because he was born with an extra chromosome, Long developed breasts during puberty, leading to his being teased mercilessly by his classmates at school.

His behavior as an adult was also negatively affected by several injuries that he suffered growing up. At the age of five, he was struck in the head. A year later, Long was flung from his bicycle when he ran into a parked car, resulting in a concussion and the loss of several teeth. Just before his marriage to his childhood sweetheart, Cindy, in 1974, Long enlisted in the army. Soon thereafter, he was involved in a motorcycle accident so serious that the impact broke his helmet and injured his skull. As a result, he was afflicted with severe headaches and violent bursts of temper for the rest of his life.

Long claimed that he developed an obsession with sex after his motorcycle accident. For a while, he was able to relieve these urges by masturbating, even after he was married. When he was unable to received satisfaction from masturbation and frequent intercourse with his wife, Long began looking for partners outside of his marriage. Around this time, Long was discharged from the army and divorced from Cindy. Between 1980 and 1983, Long found women by perusing the classified ads. He then broke into their homes and assaulted around fifty housewives while their husbands were at work in Miami, Ocala and Fort Payne. As a rule, he tied up his victims and then raped them at knifepoint. Afterward, Long stole as much as he could carry and dashed out of the house. Most of these attacks took place in midafternoon.

Around this same time, Long also strangled and shot nine women, most of whom were prostitutes. Apparently, he justified these murders by viewing his victims as nothing more than "tramps" who would never be missed by anyone.

Ironically, Long was finally apprehended as a result of his merciful treatment of one of his potential victims. On November 3, 1984, seventeen-year-old Lisa McVey was riding her bicycle home from work when suddenly, a man jumped out from behind some bushes and pulled her off her bike. To instill fear in the girl, he brandished a knife and a gun. He then forced her inside his car, where he ordered her to strip and perform oral sex on him before taking her back to his apartment. For the next twenty-six hours, he held her hostage, raping her and forcing her to take a shower with him. After he raped her, the girl told Long that she had previously been raped by her own father. To prove that she had actually been in her kidnapper's apartment, McVey dropped a barrette by the bed after he fell asleep. After waking up, he told the girl that he wished he could keep her in his apartment, away from her father. Taking her by the hand he led her to his car. He drove around for a while before pulling over and dropping her off at the curb. As he drove off, he yelled back, "Take care."

Unlike Long's other victims, McVey was able to describe him and his car, resulting in his arrest. Unfortunately, the arrest took place two days after he killed his last victim, Kim Swann. Because McVey paid close attention to her surroundings, she was able to recall that he was driving a dark red or maroon two-door Dodge Magnum with a red steering wheel. She also remembered specific details about the apartment. On November 15, two police detectives were scouring on the streets of Tampa when they noticed a red Dodge Magnum that was stuck in a traffic jam. They immediately pulled the car over to the shoulder. The man's driver's license showed that his name was Robert Joe Long and also gave his apartment address. After photographing him, the detectives released Long. When the ongoing investigation revealed that Long had been arrested in Hillsboro on aggravated battery, the detectives arrested him as he was leaving a movie theater.

The evidence against Long mounted up quickly. The investigative team assigned to Long's apartment found McVey's planted barrette, articles of women's clothing and pictures of nude women and photographs he had taken of himself raping one of his victims. When Long was confronted with this evidence and more, he said, with a smile on his face, "Well, I guess you got me good....Yes, I killed them." The transcribed version of his recorded confession was forty-five pages long. "The Classified Ad Rapist," as he became known, was sentenced to death for two of the ten murders attributed to him and was executed by lethal injection on May 23, 2019.

Christine Falling

On March 12, 1963, Ann Slaughter gave birth to a daughter, Christine, in Perry, Florida. Christine's sister, Carole, was eighteen months older. Their mother had a habit of leaving for months at a time and returning home pregnant. In the next few years, Ann gave birth to two sons, Michael and Earl. Christine and Carol's father, Thomas Slaughter, claimed that of the two boys, only Earl was his biological son. In those periods when Ann was gone, Thomas took his children to work with him in the woods. After Thomas suffered a work-related injury, Christine and her siblings lived in dire poverty. Ann returned to her family for a short while before finally abandoning her children in a shopping center.

Christine attempted to gain stability in her life by marrying a man believed to be her stepbrother when she was fourteen years old. Since she was uneducated, the only job she could find was babysitting for her friends and family members. At first glance, Christine appeared to be ideally suited for babysitting. The possibility that she was not what she appeared to be arose on February 25, 1980, when a two-year-old girl she was babysitting, Cassidy "Muffin" Johnson, became seriously ill. Later, Christine told the child's parents that the baby was injured when she fell out of her crib. Even though the child was diagnosed with encephalitis, an autopsy revealed that the little girl had died of blunt force trauma to the skull. One of her doctors expressed his opinion that Christine's role in Muffin's death should be investigated, but no further action was taken at the time.

Christine moved to Lakeland, Florida, a few weeks later. Another child she was babysitting passed away in May 1980, only two months after Christine arrived in town. Christine dialed 911, informing the operator that the four-year-old, Jeffrey Davis, had ceased breathing while in her care. Despite their best efforts, the paramedics could not resuscitate the little boy. The cause of death was officially recorded as inflammation of the heart.

Three days later, Christine was babysitting Jeffrey's cousin, two-year-old Joseph Spring, during the funeral. Once again, Christine dialed 911, stating that Joseph had stopped breathing during his nap. Later, the authorities found that Joseph had succumbed to the same viral infection as Jeffrey.

In July 1981, Christine returned to Perry, where she found employment as the housekeeper for a much older male, seventy-seven-year-old William Swindle. On Christine's first day at work, Swindle dropped dead on the kitchen floor, apparently the victim of a heart attack. Only a few weeks after his death, someone else died in Falling's care. One day, Falling rode in the car with her stepsister and her stepsister's eight-month-old baby. After a few miles, her stepsister decided to stop off at a drugstore to buy some diapers, leaving the baby in the car with Falling. When the mother opened the car door, she was shocked to find that the baby had stopped breathing and died. The cause of death was ruled an adverse reaction to a vaccination.

Death proved to be Falling's constant companion one last time on July 2, 1932, when a ten-week-old baby named Travis Coleman in her care "suddenly died," according to her testimony afterward. The week before, the little boy had been hospitalized for some sort of "respiratory illness." Falling was the child's babysitter on that day as well. A short time after the interrogation began, Falling confessed to the five murders. She admitted to killing all of them by "smotheration," a technique she claimed to have mastered by watching crime shows on television. She told the police that she added her touches to the method by placing blankets on the victims' faces and down on their mouth and nose until they stopped breathing.

At the end of her confession, the police began asking her about her involvement in the death of Coleman. She went on to elaborate on her motivation for killing each of her victims. She choked Travis to death because she was "in a bad mood that day." The only reason she could give for taking Joseph Spring's life was that she was overcome with the desire to kill. Spring "had to die" because his incessant crying was getting on Falling's nerves. Falling did not know why she killed Travis Coleman. Falling received two concurrent life sentences for three of the murders on September 17, 1982. Several years into her prison sentence, Falling finally admitted to killing William Swindle.

Flat-Tire Murders

In cases where a killer's identity has never been determined, law enforcement sometimes refers to the perpetrator by his or her modus operandi, such as the Boston Strangler or the Zodiac Killer. In the 1970s, investigators assigned the name "The Flat-Tire Murders" to a string of murders committed between February 1975 and January 1976 in Broward and Miami-Dade Counties. Judging from the evidence, investigators deduced that that the murderer was able to get close to his victims by deflating their tires in parking lots and then offering his assistance. The first two of the women murdered in Dade County in 1975 were twenty-seven-year-old Ronnie Gorlin and twenty-one-year-old Elyse Rapp. Gorlin was on her way to visit her mother at Parkway Hospital. The next day, a surveying crew found her nude body floating down the Graham Canal. Her car was found in the parking lot of a shopping center. A tire had been slashed. Elyse Rapp vanished after going to a shopping mall. Investigators reported that when her car turned up in the mall parking lot, they found that one of its tires was also flat. Her nude body was also found in the Graham Canal. She had been raped and hit on the head. The discovery of the bodies of two young women in the same canal led investigators to conclude that that a serial killer was on the loose.

The next two victims were dumped in the canal running along Miami-Dade and Broward Counties. Twenty-year-old masseuse Judith Ann Oesterling was driving from the massage parlor, but she never made it home.

Two days later, her nude body was discovered floating in the canal. The body of a seventeen-year-old-divorcée named Arietta Tinker was found floating in the canal a few days later, not far from where Oesterling's body was discovered.

The murderer's next victim was from a relatively privileged background. Twenty-one-year-old Barbara Davis Stephens, the daughter of the president of the Aurora Electric Company, was traveling to Coral Gables to visit a friend. Instigators later determined that she had purchased several records at a Golden Triangle store before her family lost contact with her. Her murderer appeared to have stabbed her several times and then transported her corpse to a heavily wooded dump.

Nineteen-year-old Nancy Fox became another victim of the mysterious assailant. Discouraged by her involvement in an unhappy love triangle involving herself, her sister and William Moore Jr., she relocated to Fort Lauderdale in 1975 to make a new start for herself. She was reported missing while walking to an unknown destination. Like that of several of the other women, her body was thrown into a canal; this one was parallel to Highway 27 in Broward County. A convicted rapist named Walter Wirth and William Moore Jr. were suspects in the case, but neither man was charged with her murder.

The next two victims also disappeared while walking. Barbara Susan Schreiber and Belinda Darlene Zetterower, both fourteen years old, were on their way to their friend Valerie's house, where they had planned to spend the night. A family who was fishing in the canal parallel to Highway 27 made a gruesome discovery a couple of days later when they came upon the bodies of two girls lying on the bank. Both of them had been shot, probably at the site where their bodies had been placed. The body of another fourteen-year-old, Robin Leslie Losch, was found in the Highway 27 canal on February 14. Although the detectives were certain that the girl had drowned, they were unable to determine whether or not she had been the victim of foul play.

The killer's last possible victims in 1975 were Mary Coppola, fourteen, and Marlene Annabelli, twenty-seven. They had traveled from Pennsylvania to Fort Lauderdale. They paid for a week's stay at the Lauderdale Beach Club. Nine days later, a motorcyclist found their bodies in a dump on the city limits.

The last victim attributed to the Flat-Tire Killer was seventeen-year-old Michelle Winters. At the time of her disappearance, she seemed to be upset about something, according to her friends, who assumed that she was planning to enlist in the navy. When her body was discovered on January 11,

1976, in Snapper Creek in Pembroke Pines, some investigators speculated that Ted Bundy may have been the murderer, but no evidence has surfaced to support that allegation.

An article on the website Cold Case Project suggests that the Flat-Tire Murderer may have been active in other states before coming to Florida. In the article, police sergeant Edwin Carlstedt theorized that the murderer started killing women in California in 1973 and continued his murder spree in Washington, Idaho, Utah and Colorado. Carlstedt based his theory on the killer's modus operandi in over thirty-five murders, as well as the similarities between the victims. As of yet, no one has ever been found guilty of any of the murders.

EDDIE LEE MOSLEY

Born on March 31, 1947, in Fort Lauderdale, Eddie Lee Mosley had a childhood plagued with problems. He developed respiratory problems from complications at birth. Several mental problems, including anterograde amnesia, mental instability and intellectual disability, became evident when he was a small child. In 1960, he was removed from school permanently in the third grade when he was thirteen years old, primarily because of his antisocial behavior. Because he was illiterate, Mosley was qualified only for low-paying menial jobs. He was arrested for disorderly conduct in 1965 when he was eighteen years old. Following this arrest—his first—Mosley was arrested nine other times for crimes such as armed robbery, indecent proposal, sexual assault and murder.

Most of the crimes Mosley was charged with in the early 1970s were of a sexual nature. He was finally apprehended on July 23, 1973, when three women seated in a police car driving along Northwest Thirty-First Avenue, recognized him. They were able to identify him because of his large stature and his noticeable limp and facial scar. He was not charged with the murders of two Black women in 1973; instead, police charged Jerry Frank Townsend with the crimes. Accused of assault and rape, Mosley was committed to the Florida State Hospital for five years. During his confinement, the number of rapes similar to the ones he was charged with declined.

On February 1, 1979, Mosley was transferred to the Florida State Hospital. He was discharged after only five months of treatment because he was found to be "cured." Mosley returned to his parents' house to live. During the next seven months, seven Black women were raped and murdered. To shield him from the police, who were making inquiries, his parents sent him to his grandmother's house in Lakeland. After several weeks, the bodies of two Black women were discovered. Mosley's crime spree came to a temporary halt when he was arrested on April 12, 1980, for the attempted rape of a girl. At the end of the ensuing trial, Mosley was found guilty and sentenced to fifteen years in prison. Because of his lawyer's incompetence, Mosley's conviction was overturned three years later. He was paroled on December 15, 1983.

Mosley was a free man for just a few months. In May 17, 1984, he was accused of raping a twenty-two-year-old woman but was released after convincing a jury that she had agreed to have sex with him in exchange for drugs. During his arrest on drug charges, authorities found that his blood group aligned with samples taken from murder scenes not far from his house. He attempted to provide an alibi, but it was so garbled that he finally gave up and admitted that he had murdered Teresa Giles and Emma Cook. At the end of his trial, which was held on July 22, 1981, he was sentenced once again to Florida State Hospital.

Thanks to DNA testing conducted in 2000, he was found guilty of the murders of Loretta Young Brown, Vetta Turner, Sonya Marion, Terri Jean Cummings, Emma Cook and Teresa Giles. However, because psychiatric tests indicated that he was insane, Mosley could not be imprisoned. He was transferred to the Sunland Center in Marianna because of his mounting health problems. Mosley died of COVID-19 on May 28, 2020. He was seventy-three years old.

DANNY ROLLING

Born on March 26, 1954, Danny was the product of an abusive home life. His father, a policeman named James Rolling, seems to have hated his son because he was conceived before his parents' marriage. James began beating the boy when he was crawling. He frequently told Danny that he was an unwanted child. When Danny was older, his father handcuffed the boy and had a couple of his police friends take him to the station because the boy "embarrassed him." James also abused his wife, Cynthia, even forcing her to cut her arm with a razor blade. She left him on several occasions, but she always came back home. Even the family dog became the target of James's wrath. In fact, he beat the poor animal so often that it finally died in Danny's arms. In May 1990, Danny's father pushed him too far. In a fit of rage, Danny shot the man in his stomach and his eye. James survived but lost an eye.

Not surprisingly, Danny became a troubled youth in his late teenage years and throughout his twenties. While living in Georgia, Danny was arrested several times on robbery charges. He was also accused of peeping at a cheerleader while she was changing her clothes. During this stage in his life, he held down a variety of odd jobs, including a short stint as a waiter at Pancho's Restaurant in Shreveport, Louisiana.

Not long after attacking his father, Danny embarked on a bloody crime spree in Gainesville, Florida. On August 24, Danny forced his way inside an apartment rented by two seventeen-year-olds, Sonja Larson and Christine Powell. While Powell was sleeping on the couch downstairs, Danny walked past her and climbed the stairs to Larson's room. He taped her mouth shut and stabbed her with his Ka-Bar knife. After he was certain that Larson was dead, Danny returned downstairs where Powell was still asleep. He cut the girl with his knife and raped her before stabbing her five times in the back, killing her. Danny arranged their corpses in erotic postures before exiting the apartment.

The next day, Rolling broke into eighteen-year-old Christa Hoyt's apartment by opening the lock on the glass door with his knife and a screwdriver. Hoyt had not yet returned to the apartment, so Rolling waited for her. When she finally walked through the door, he sneaked up behind her and threw her on the floor. After raping her, Rolling thrust his knife in her back so hard that it ruptured her heart. Before leaving the apartment, Rolling cut off her head and placed it on a shelf facing her corpse, which he had placed on the bed in a sitting position.

Rolling committed his final murder two days later. Alarmed by the senseless murders of the other three girls, Tracy Paules asked her roommate, Manny Taboada, to keep watch for intruders during the night. Sometime after midnight, Rolling forced his way into the apartment using the same tools as before. Surprised to find that Paules was not alone, Rolling struggled with Taboada before finally stabbing him to death. Rolling then turned his attention to Paules, who was hiding in her room, which she had attempted to barricade shut. Enraged, Rolling forced the door open and raped her. After taping her mouth shut, Rolling cut off her clothes and stabbed her in the back three times. He left Taboada lying on the floor, but he posed Paules's corpse.

The Gainesville police initially focused their investigation on a college student with intellectual disabilities named Edward Humphrey. Around the same time, the real murderer, Danny Rolling, was arrested on burglary charges after the police identified his knife and screwdriver as the tools that had been used in the break-ins as the crime scene. Convinced that Rolling was the "Gainesville Ripper," as the killer was now known, the authorities released Humphrey and formally charged Rolling with the murders in 1991.

Following Rolling's arrest, the police department in Shreveport, Louisiana, fingered Rolling as the prime suspect in the triple homicide of the Grissom family, who were killed while getting dinner ready. The department's interest in Rolling was heightened by the fact that Julia Grissom's corpse was desecrated and posed, just like the bodies of Rolling's victims in Gainesville. Rolling also knew information about the Grissom killings that only the murderer could have known. The lead investigator in the Gainesville murders, Don Maines, was encouraged by Rolling's possible connection to the Shreveport murders, which he believed strengthened the case against him. He was indicted of five counts of first-degree murder in November 1991. The charges were based primarily on DNA evidence.

When Rolling's trial began on February 15, 1994, the authorities expected it to last six months. However, Rolling surprised everyone by confessing to murders on the first day, although he never took credit for the Grissom murders. The trial immediately entered its penalty phase, during which Rolling stated that he wanted to be a "superstar," like Ted Bundy. He was sentence to death on each count. On October 25, 2005, Rolling was executed by lethal injection. Today, he is remembered as the serial killer who inspired the movie *Scream*.

GERARD SCHAEFER

Born on March 25, 1946, in Neenah, Wisconsin, Gerard Schaefer was the oldest of his two siblings. He and his siblings were raised in Nashville, Tennessee, and Atlanta, Georgia. In 1960, Schaefer and his family made their permanent home in Fort Lauderdale, Florida. His father, a traveling salesman, was an alcoholic who verbally abused his wife and children. From all appearances, though, Schaefer had a normal childhood. However, like many serial killers, he enjoyed killing small animals. In statements he made to a psychiatrist in 1966, Schaefer admitted that he was sexually confused as a boy. When he was young, he experienced gender envy because of his father's favoritism toward his sister. During this period in his life, he found himself longing to be a girl. He also said that he was given to bouts of sadomasochism beginning at the age of twelve. Not only did he fantasize about hurting and torturing other people, especially women, but he also tied himself to trees and struggled to escape, thereby achieving sexual satisfaction.

In his twenties, Schaefer explored several different career options. He became disenchanted with Catholicism after being rejected for the priesthood. Afterward, Schaefer was appointed to a teaching position, but he was fired for attempting to impose his own moral views on his students. Around this time, Schaefer married Martha Fogg, but they divorced two years later.

After vacationing in Europe and North Africa, Schaefer embarked on his third career choice: law enforcement. He was hired by the Wilton Manors Police Department, and he started out with a commendation in March 1972 for a drug bust. However, he was fired soon thereafter for asking several female traffic violators out on dates. In June 1972, the Martin County Sheriff's Department hired him. On July 21, his career as a policemen came to an end. He arrested two young girls—Pamela Wells, seventeen, and Nancy Trotter, eighteen—on the charge of hitchhiking to the beach. Schaefer offered to drive them to the beach. They had just gone as far as Hutchinson Island when Schaefer stopped the car and turned off the engine. Brandishing his pistol, he ordered the girls to exit the car. He then tied them to a tree and placed a hangman's noose around their necks. Before driving off, he told the girls he would return shortly. As soon as his car was out of sight, the girls made their escape. When he returned and discovered the girls were missing, he called the station and admitted to Sheriff Robert that he had "done something very foolish." Schaefer was fired on the spot and charged with one count of false imprisonment and two counts of aggravated assault. He pleaded guilty to one charge of assault—the other two counts were dropped—and was sentenced to one year in prison and three years' probation.

Schaefer's fondness for abducting young women continued, despite the loss of his career. On September 27, 1972, while he was free on bond pending trial, Schaefer met two girls—seventeen-year-old Susan Place and sixteen-year-old Georgia Jessup—while walking through an adult education center in Fort Lauderdale. He introduced himself to them as Jerry Shephard. He ingratiated himself with the girls by sharing his interest in ESP, reincarnation and music. That afternoon, Schaefer picked up the girls at Place's parents' house and told them that they were going to the beach to "play guitar." Before they left, Place's mother wrote down the license plate number on "Shephard's" car. Four days later, Mrs. Place contacted Jessup's mother, who said that Georgia had run away on September 27. Both women reported their daughters missing to the Oakland Park Police Department, which traced the plate number to Schaefer, who had been arrested for molesting teenage girls.

Schaefer told the police that he had no connection at all to the two girls. However, he became the prime suspect on April 1, 1973, after three men collecting aluminum cans on Hutchinson Island made a grisly find in a hole dug in a wooded area in Oak Hammock Park in Port St. Lucie, Florida: the bones of two different people. Using dental records and healed bone fractures, Dr. Richard Souviron identified the remains as being those of Place and Jessup on April 5. Six days later, police got a permit to investigate the bedroom in his mother's house where he had been storing some of his personal possessions. The evidence they found included women's jewelry, sketches of the butchered bodies of women, and several typed stories of the abduction, rape and murder of several teenage girls, two of whom he identified as "Belinda" and "Carmen." In addition, investigators found newspaper articles concerning the disappearance of two nineteen-year-old hitchhikers: Collette Goodenough and Barbara Wilcox. Investigators also found a gold locket bearing the inscribed name "Leigh," which may have belonged to Schaefer's neighbor Leigh Hainline Bonadies, who went missing as well. On May 12, investigators announced that they had information linking Schaefer with nine murders committed between 1969 and 1973, but he was charged only with the deaths of Place and Jessup.

Schaefer's trial began on September 17, 1973, in St. Lucie County. The presiding judge was Cyrus Pfeiffer Trowbridge. Schaefer maintained his innocence throughout the trial. In October 1973, he was found guilty and given two life sentences. The prosecuting attorney, Robert Stone, later said that Schaefer was "the most sexually deviant person I had ever seen." For the next twenty-two years, Schaefer filed a number of appeals and frivolous lawsuits, all of which were rejected. His tendency to "narc" on his fellow inmates and threaten them with violence made him unpopular in his cell block. On December 3, 1995, a fellow inmate named Vincent Rivera stabbed him to death in his cell. He was found guilty of Schaefer's murder, and another fifty-three years were added to his twenty-year-sentence.

AILEEN WUORNOS

On February 29, 1956, Aileen Carol Pittman was born to Diane Pratt and Leo Dale Pittman in Rochester, Michigan. He was not a prominent figure in his daughter's life, because as a child molester, he spent a great deal of time in prison before finally being strangled to death while incarcerated in 1969. Almost two years after her marriage to Pittman, Diane divorced him. Diane turned over Wuornos and her brother, Keith, to her parents in 1960. While living with her grandparents, Wuornos was molested by her grandfather and his friend, who impregnated her. She gave birth to a son, whom she gave up for adoption. She went to have sex with a number of different men as an adolescent, including her brother, Keith. For a while, she was forced to leave her grandparents' home and live in the woods.

Once she became an adult, Wuornos hitchhiked from place to place, earning her living as a sex worker. Following her arrest for disorderly conduct and assault, in the mid-1970s, Wuornos moved to Florida, where she met and married a rich man named Lewis Fell in 1976, but he annulled the marriage after a short while.

For the next ten years, Wuornos was charged with a series of criminal offenses, including grand theft auto, assault, armed robbery and the theft of a gun. In 1986, she became romantically involved with twenty-five-year-old Tyria Moore, who worked as a maid in a Daytona hotel. Wuornos resorted to prostitution to support the two of them. By 1980, Wuornos began picking up men in truck stops and bars, occasionally resorting to theft when she had difficulty finding "customers." At this time, Wuornos's behavior became erratic, occasion erupting into violent outbursts. By the end of the decade, Wuornos had murdered at least six men, beginning on November 30, 1989, and continuing into the fall of 1990. The body of the first of her victims, a hard-drinking, porn-loving electrician from Palm Harbor, Richard Mallory, was discovered in a heavily wooded area northwest of Daytona Beach. His murderer had shot him three times in the chest. The bodies of more men were found in various places along Florida highways in the next few months. On June 3, 1990, the badly decomposed body of forty-three-year-old David Spears was found in the woods approximately forty miles north of Tampa. He had been shot six times with a .22-caliber weapon. Thirty miles south of the place where Spears's body was discovered, the body of a forty-year-old rodeo worker named Charles Carskaddon was found around the same time as the discovery of Spears's corpse. He had been shot nine times by a .22-caliber weapon. Police found another decomposed body on August 4, 1990. It was later identified as the body of a fifty-year-old salesman named Troy Buress. He had been shot twice in the torso. On September 12, 1990, the body of a retired police chief and child abuse investigator was found in Marion County. His attacker had shot him several times in the head. The body of a sixty-five-year-old merchant seaman, Peter Siems, was found in Orange Springs on July 4, 1990. Two women were seen in the vicinity of the car by several witnesses. The half-naked body of sixty-two-year-old Walter Antonio was discovered in Dixie County. He had been shot in the back and the head.

The identity of the assailant was unknown until the fingerprints and palm print found in Siems's car were identified as belonging to Wuornos and Moore. While searching through pawnshops in the area, police found Wuornos's thumbprint on objects stolen from Richard Mallory. Moore's growing concern about Wuornos's "other activities" led her to return to her family home in Pennsylvania. Meanwhile, Wuornos traveled to Harbor Oaks, Florida, where she was apprehended in a biker bar. Not long thereafter, authorities trailed Moore to Florida and made a deal with her. Moore agreed to talk Wuornos into confessing. During a telephone conversation, Wuornos admitted that she alone killed all those men. On January 14, 1992, Wuornos was tried for the murder of Richard Mallory. She testified that she had murdered Mallory because he had raped her. She was found guilty of first-degree murder and received the death penalty on January 27, 1992. While awaiting execution, Wuornos confessed to killing the five other men and received the death penalty for each murder. Even though she took responsibility for Siems's murder, she was not indicted because his body was never found.

Over the next decade, Wuornos fired her appeal lawyers. Her brash behavior troubled a court-appointed lawyer, who convinced a judge that she was mentally unstable. In 2002, Governor Jeb Bush reversed her stay of execution and declared her mentally capable of understanding the reason why she had received the death penalty. During the trial, Wuornos claimed to still be in love with Tyria Moore. On October 9, 2002, she was executed by lethal injection.

Since her execution, Aileen Wuornos's life and crimes have been kept alive in the media. She has been the subject of a number of books, including Aileen Wuornos's *Dear Dawn: Aileen Wuornos in Her Own Words* (2012), Aileen Wuornos's and Christopher Berry-Dee's *Monster: My True Story* (2004), Michael Reynolds's *Dead Ends* (1992), Sue Russell's *Lethal Intent*

(2002). Documentaries about Aileen Wuornos include *Aileen Wuornos: The Selling of a Serial Killer* (1993) and *Aileen: Life and Death of a Serial Killer* (2003). Films include *Monster* (2003), for which Charlize Theron won the Academy Award for Best Actress, and *Aileen Wuornos: American Boogeyman* (2021). Poetry inspired by Wuornos includes Rim Banerji's "Sugar Zero" (2005), Doron Braunsfcin's "Aileen Wuornos," and Olivia Gatewood's book of poetry *Life of the Party* (2019). Music that has been influenced by Wuornos includes Carl Lucero's opera *Wuornos*, Jewel's song "Nicotine Love," Superhaven's "Poor Aileen" and Sadistik's song "Aileen Wuornos."

8

STRANGE BURIALS AND CEMETERIES

CAPTAIN TONY'S SALOON (KEY WEST)

The building at 428 Green Street served two purposes when it was constructed between 1851 and 1852. Because it was an icehouse, it was an ideal location for the city morgue as well. The bodies of indigent people were buried in an open yard next door to the morgue. When a powerful hurricane surged through Key West in the summer of 1865, a number of bodies in the makeshift potter's field washed to the surface. After the bodies were reburied in the potter's field, a wall was built around it, and holy water was sprinkled around the graves to sanctify them. Around the turn of the century, the building became a radio station. It was from this site that the news of the sinking of the battleship *Maine* was first broadcast around the world.

In the twentieth century, the building was repurposed a number of times. A cigar factory was housed there in 1912. A few years later, a bordello moved in, followed by a bar. During the Prohibition era in the 1920s, several different speakeasies operated from the building, including one with the colorful name the Blind Pig, which offered patrons gambling and prostitutes as well as bootleg rum. Around this time, an enterprising businessman named Josie "Sloppy Joe" Russell leased the building toward the end of the decade in the hope that Prohibition would end soon. After the repeal of Prohibition on December 5, 1933, Russell opened up Sloppy Joe's bar in 1933. One of

Captain Tony's Saloon, writer Ernest Hemingway's favorite watering hole, contains a couple of tombstones, including one belonging to an unfaithful wife. *Wikimedia Commons.*

his best patrons was the writer Ernest Hemingway. The building changed hands over the next couple of decades. Then in 1959, a charter boat captain named Tony Tarricino purchased the original Sloppy Joe's and gave it his own name: Captain Tony's Saloon. Captain Tony sold the bar in 1989 in order to pursue his dream of becoming mayor of Key West. He died in 2008. Today, Sloppy Joe's is not only known as Ernest Hemingway's former "watering hole" but also for the famous musical artists who have performed there, such as Jimmy Buffett and Bob Dylan. The legends that Captain Tony regaled his customers with also attracted people to Sloppy Joe's/Captain Tony's Saloon.

One of the stories Captain Tony told was that some of the corpses that were washed out of their graves by a hurricane in 1865 were buried under the place where the poolroom now stands. Supposedly, he filled bottles with holy water and embedded them in the walls of the poolroom to keep the spirits quiet. This "wild story" received some credibility in the 1980s when workmen excavating under the south floor found around a dozen skeletons. Captain Tony liked to tell his customers that a skeleton composed of the

The ceiling of Captain Tony's Saloon is lined with bras donated by patrons over the years. *Wikimedia Commons.*

bones of three different bodies was buried behind the bar. He claimed to have found the bones in a dry well next to the saloon.

Interestingly enough, a couple of tombstones can be found in Captain Tony's Saloon as well. At the bottom of the hanging tree is the tombstone of Reba Sawyer. When she died in 1950, she was buried in Key West Cemetery. Not long after the funeral, her husband was going through her belongings when he found a pack of letters his wife had written to her lover. While reading through the letters, he found out that Reba and her boyfriend had their rendezvous at Captain Tony's saloon. The story goes that the enraged husband carted his cheating wife's tombstone into Captain Tony's and placed it under the hanging tree. With sweat dripping from his brow, he exclaimed, "Here is where she wanted to be. Here is where she will stay!"

Legend has it that the same workmen who uncovered the bones under the floor in the 1980s also found the tombstone of a woman named Elvira Edmond. This tombstone was placed on the floor of the billiards room. Over time, her name was attached to the woman who was hanged from the bar's hanging tree in 1822. As the building expanded, it was built around an old tree from which an assortment of scoundrels, including pirates, were hanged.

The Huguenot Cemetery (St. Augustine)

During the Spanish occupation of the Florida territory, all of the cemeteries in St. Augustine were predominately Catholic. However, following the signing of the Adams-Onís Treaty of 1819, ceding all of Spanish-held Florida to America, the establishment of a Protestant cemetery in St. Augustine became a necessity. In 1821, a plot of land across from the Old City Gates was set aside for the new cemetery, just before a yellow fever epidemic claimed hundreds of lives in the area. In 1832, the Presbyterian Church took possession of the cemetery after it was purchased by the Reverend Thomas Alexander. By the time the cemetery closed in 1884, 436 bodies had been buried there. In spite of its name, Huguenot Cemetery, no members of the French Protestant group are among the people buried here. Today, the Huguenot Cemetery is reputed to be one of the most haunted cemeteries in the entire state.

The most high-profile of the ghosts in the cemetery is the spirit of a local magistrate named Judge Stickney. A native of New York, Stickney fought in the Civil War before finally settling in St. Augustine, where he became the state's attorney for the Sixth Judicial Circuit of Florida. When the judge died in 1882, he was remembered as a generous man who dispensed legal advice at no charge, on occasion. Years later, his adult children decided to have their father's body exhumed and reburied in Washington, D.C. The story goes that on the day in 1903 when his body was to be exhumed, the gravediggers were surprised to find when they returned from their lunch break that several grave robbers were inside the open grave, probing around for valuables. As soon as the thieves caught sight of the men, they took off, leaving their shovels behind. Unfortunately, the ghouls were able to make off with a few of the judge's possessions, including his gold teeth.

The desecration of Judge Stickney's grave and body has given rise to a great deal of persistent paranormal activity. Judge Stickney's restless apparition has been sighted sitting in the boughs of a tree and strolling around the tombstones, with his head down. Some believe he is looking for his pilfered teeth. Visitors have reported hearing the unmistakable sound of someone walking through the dry leaves when no one was present.

Another ghost who has been frequently sighted in the Huguenot Cemetery is the spirit of a fourteen-year-old girl who died of yellow fever in 1821. For some unknown reason, her corpse was left outside of the Old City Gates. Even though her body was buried inside the cemetery, her spirit has not yet acclimated itself to its new surroundings. Her ghost, wearing a flowing white gown, has been seen floating around the trees, usually between midnight and 2:00 a.m.

The girl's ghost or the ghost of Judge Stickney might be responsible for the high levels of paranormal activity in the Huguenot Cemetery. A number of paranormal investigators have captured unnerving images of shining orbs and flashes of light, as well as shadowy figures and misty shapes. The spirits also seem to enjoy manifesting through sound, such as the rustling of bushes or spectral laughter. For many visitors, the Huguenot Cemetery seems to be a good place to make contact with the "other side."

I-4 DEAD ZONE
(BETWEEN ORLANDO AND DAYTONA)

In most cultures, burial sites are sacred places. American folklore is filled with cautionary tales about interlopers who did not respect the final resting place of the dear departed. A good example is the Mississippi Coast Coliseum and Convention Center, which was built in 1977 over the cemetery of an orphanage that once stood on this location. As a result, a great deal of paranormal activity has been reported here. Sometimes, highways built on holy ground are haunted as well, such as Interstate 4 between Orland and Daytona in Florida.

According to the website toptenz.net, the land under what is now the St. John's River Bridge was nothing more than an a heavily wooded area with a sand road. Toward the end of the nineteenth century, the owner of the land, Henry Sanford, set about establishing a Roman Catholic colony named St. Joseph's Colony on his property after a railroad station was located there in 1886. He was expecting a large influx of German immigrants, but only four German families showed up. When an outbreak of yellow fever swept the area in the early 1887, their corpses were cremated in the woods to stave off infecting the other families. The local priest left the colony to tend to the yellow fever victims in Tampa, but he, too, contracted the disease three days later and passed away. Consequently, the ashes of the first four victims were buried with very little ceremony.

By 1890, the threat of yellow fever was beginning to wane, enabling St. Joseph's Colony to grow into a town called Lake Monroe. A farmer purchased the land on which the four victims were buried. However, in an effort to show respect for the dead, he planted around the graves. In 1905, Albert

S. Hawkins bought the farmland. The penalty for dishonoring the buried dead became readily apparent after a farmer who was renting the land from Hawkins removed the fence encircling the graves. A few days later, his house burned down. Hawkins's home, located on the edge of a field, caught fire and burned as well. He rebuilt his house after restoring the grave markers that someone had removed, but after he and his family moved in, the tranquility of their new home was interrupted by a great deal of poltergeist activity, such as toys that moved on their own and eerie balls of light that passersby claimed to have seen around the grave site. Stories about the presence of spirits around the graves seemed to be substantiated by the fate of a boy who was killed by a drunk driver shortly after vandalizing the graves.

In 1959, the property was purchased by the state for the purpose of constructing Interstate 4 through it. Instead of relocating the graves, state authorities decided to pour dirt over them to elevate the roadway. Around that time, Hurricane Donna did extensive damage to this spot on September 10, 1960, causing construction to be delayed for a month. In 2004, Hurricane Charley veered from the path it was taking and also set down on the graves of the four German immigrants.

Since the completion of the interstate, a large number of strange occurrences have taken place on this 132-mile stretch of highway. Travelers say they have picked up the spectral voices of children asking questions like "Who's there?" and "Why?" through their cellphones while passing through the south end of the Interstate 4 Bridge. Drivers have sighted a strange mist and glowing orbs floating in an erratic pattern over the interstate. A few people have reported that some sort of force took control of their car on the interstate. Perhaps this is the reason why an unusually high number of accidents have occurred on Interstate 4. It is no wonder that Interstate 4 has been called one of the most haunted highways in the United States.

OLD CITY CEMETERY (TALLAHASSEE)

Established in 1829 on a former cattle farm outside of the city boundaries, Old City Cemetery is the oldest public graveyard in Tallahassee. White people were buried on the eastern half of the cemetery while enslaved and free people of color were buried on the western half. Following a yellow fever epidemic in 1841, the city took control of the cemetery to meet the growing need for burial space. As time passed, the cemetery became the

One of the many historic graves in Tallahassee's Old City Cemetery is that of Major General David Lang, adjutant general of Florida (1885–1894). *Wikimedia Commons.*

final resting place for Tampa's most illustrious and lesser-known citizens, including planters, slaves, governors, war veterans and victims of yellow fever. In the early years, the graves were often trampled on by hogs and cattle, which were attracted to the cemetery by the tall grass that grew everywhere. To make matters worse, the carts transporting bodies to the cemetery also damaged the graves. The neglect continued until the 1980s, when rampant vandalism made it clear that the historic cemetery was in dire need of attention. The installation of a wrought-iron fence around the cemetery signaled the completion of the reconditioning process. The most visited grave is that of Elizabeth "Bessie" Budd-Graham, undoubtedly the most legendary occupant of Tallahassee's Old City Cemetery.

Elizabeth Budd-Graham was a twenty-three-year-old wife and mother when she died in 1880. She was married to a rich "lumber baron" named Joan A. Graham. Not long after her death, an elaborate obelisk was erected on her grave, and Elizabeth became the subject of a variety of stories, most of which were untrue. The fact that her headstone faces west instead of east raised suspicions among many people. This violation of Christian tradition created a sinister aura around her grave. Because Elizabeth died in October, some of Tampa's more superstitious citizens connected the time of her death with the occult. The inscription of lines of a poem from Edgar Allan Poe's "Lenore" also led people to speculate that she might have dabbled in witchcraft: "Ah, broken is the golden bowl! the spirit flown forever! / Let the bell toll!—a saintly soul floats on the Stygian river." One interpretation of these lines is that Elizabeth is doomed to spend eternity in limbo because witches are unable to cross the River Styx. Rumors quickly spread that Elizabeth was actually a good witch who had cast a love spell on the man who became her husband. According to the blog oldcityghosts.com, most of the supposed occult evidence on the tombstone can be explained away logically. In the Victorian era, many people were buried facing the west to represent the "setting sun" (in other words, death). The abundance of Christian imagery on the tombstone negates the possibility that Elizabeth was a witch. Nevertheless, the legend of the witch of the Old City Cemetery attracts hundreds of curiosity seekers and self-appointed witches who practice rituals and leave offerings to Elizabeth in the hope that their coins and seashells will bring them luck.

This elaborate monument in Tallahassee's Old City Cemetery is said to mark the grave of Elizabeth Budd-Graham, who is believed to have been a witch. *Wikimedia Commons.*

Pinewood Cemetery (Daytona Beach)

Pinewood Cemetery was established on land bought by an immigrant from Canada, John W. Smith, in 1873. Even though he advertised lots for sale in 1883, the first burial was the daughter of Smith's nineteen-year-old daughter. In the early 1900s, Charles Bingham and Jerome Maley, the owners of a furniture/undertaking establishment, decided to expand their business interests by forming the Pinewood Cemetery Corporation. They started out by erecting archways and coquina walls. By 1917, they were selling lots for fifty dollars apiece. The corporation's maintenance fund was lost in the Great Depression. Consequently, the cemetery suffered from neglect and vandalism for almost fifty years. No one has been buried in Pinewood Cemetery since the early 1970s. Today, the cemetery is kept up primarily through money left in trust by Albert Kingston, who died in 1979 and is buried in Pinewood Cemetery. The bikers from the Boot Hill Saloon across the street also lend a hand in keeping the cemetery clean. Today, Pinewood Cemetery is remembered not just as the oldest cemetery in Daytona Beach but also as the setting of some scary ghost stories.

One of these tales harkens back to John W. Smith, the founder of Pinewood Cemetery. In 1853, Smith settled on the property that is now the cemetery. According to Dusty Smith, author of *Haunted Daytona Beach*, he set aside four and a half acres of his homestead as a wedding present for his daughter, Alena Beatrice. He named the plot of land "Memento." The story goes that when she became a teenager, she talked her father into mounding up dirt on the plot of the land so that she could see the ocean. By the time Alena was nineteen years old, she would often walk up the hill and daydream about the beautiful wedding she would have some day and the fine house she and her future husband would build there. Alena's dreams of marital bliss came to a rather abrupt end on April 15, 1877, when she contracted smallpox and died. Smith buried her in her white batiste wedding gown on the spot that she had envisioned as the site of her new home, making her the first occupant in what came to be known as Pinewood Cemetery. People in the 1920s reported seeing the figure of a woman in long, white batiste dress floating around the cemetery. Most of the sightings have taken place on April 15, the anniversary of Alena's death.

A headless ghost is said to haunt the cemetery as well. In the 1950s, a group of boys made Alder Rawlings's tomb their clubhouse after the police forced them to abandon their hangout on the boardwalk. Alder Rawlings was a prominent figure in the history of Daytona Beach. According to an article published on the *Free Press* website—"Graveyard Ghosts: Headless Spirt Roams the Pinewood Cemetery in Daytona Beach"—the boys used Rawlings' coffin as their meeting table. As their membership grew, the boys decided that they needed more space, so they removed the coffin from the tomb and threw the casket into the road. Legend has it that the body fell out of the coffin, and the head fell off. The police put the body back into the casket, but the head had disappeared. Some locals believe that members of the club made off with Rawlings's head. Police placed Rawlings's headless corpse back in his coffin and returned it to the tomb. The entrance to the tomb was sealed with large cement blocks to prevent anyone else from entering the tomb. For years, many people have claimed to see a headless man walking through the cemetery. In most of these reports, he is said to be looking for his lost head. In a totally unrelated ghost story, the cats in the cemetery, which are provided with food, water and shelter, are believed to play with the spirits.

St. Paul's Cathedral Cemetery (Key West)

In 1831, the city council of Key West held a public meeting to explore the possibility of erecting an Episcopal church in Key West. The bishop of New York was contacted, and the first rector, Reverend Samson K. Brunot, arrived on December 23, 1832. The county courthouse served as the site of the first service on December 24, 1832. The widow of landowner John William Charles Fleming donated the land for a permanent church building. The first church, built of coral rock, was completed in 1839. After the church was destroyed by a hurricane on October 11, 1846, it was replaced in 1848 with a wooden building. The Right Reverend C.E. Gadsden consecrated the church on January 4, 1851. In March 1886, the Great Fire of Key West destroyed the second church. Within a year, a new wooden structure was built on the site of the previous church. A new chime of bells was installed in 1891. The third incarnation of the church was destroyed in 1909. Services were held in the two surviving church buildings—the parish hall and the rectory—until the new church was constructed on the corner of Duval and Eaton Streets between 1919 and 1920. By 1991, the rigors of time and the weather necessitated a major restoration. Work was completed in 1993 at the cost of almost $1 million. Right Reverend Peter Eaton, bishop of

Southeast Florida, presided over the mass celebrating the 199th anniversary of the church on February 2, 2020.

Most of the ghostly activity at St. Paul's is said to occur in and around the cemetery behind the church. The most commonly sighted apparition is a misty, vaporous figure wearing a nineteenth-century suit that walks through the graveyard. Some people believe that this is the ghost of John Fleming, who cannot rest because the exact site of his grave has never been located. A much more belligerent specter is the ghost of a sea captain. Visitors to the graveyard who attempted to sit by his grave claim that a few minutes later the leaves of a nearby tree were stirred up by a strong wind, even on calm days. The sea captain's apparition has also been known to scare away people who visit the small garden outside of the cemetery.

The cemetery's most tragic ghosts are the spirits of several small children. Legend has it that one day in the late 1800s, a man attempted to burn down the church when he learned that the pastor was having an affair with his wife. He was totally unaware that several children were in the church at the time. The children perished when the flames raged through the church. Many people have seen their small ghosts clinging to the statue of the angel in the center of the cemetery. Other people say that they gather around cemeteries bearing the engraved images of angels.

Tolomato Cemetery (St. Augustine)

Tolomato Cemetery on Cordova Street in St. Augustine is the oldest planned cemetery in the United States. Its name is derived from a Guale Indian mission that was once located on this site during the First Spanish period. These converts to Christianity were ministered to by Franciscan friars. From the eighteenth century up to the cemetery's closing in 1884, approximately one thousand people from Greece, Cuba, Ireland Minorca, Italy, Africa, Haiti, France and the American South and Northeast were buried here, as well as Union and Confederate soldiers. Some of the most fascinating aspects of this historic cemetery are the stories that were left behind.

One of the saddest tales concerns a five-year-old boy named James who, like many children in the area, viewed the graveyard as his personal playground. He was especially fond of climbing the tallest oak tree in the entire cemetery. One day in January 1877, James was scaling the tree when he lost his footing and fell to the ground below. His mother became

The ghost of a five-year-old boy has been seen sitting in his favorite tree in Tolomato Cemetery. *Wikimedia Commons.*

concerned when her little boy did not return home at his appointed time. She walked through cemetery gate and went directly to James's tree. Her heart caught in her throat when she spotted a small figure lying facedown at the foot of the tree. James's love for the tree was so strong that his mother persuaded the local priest to allow her to bury her son on the very place where he fell. Until the day she died, she swore that she occasionally saw her son's ghost sitting on the branches at the top of the tree. Although some people may have claimed to see James's ghost to humor his mother, a photograph taken several years ago shows what appears to be a small child sitting in the tree.

The most prestigious person to be buried in Tolomato Cemetery was Bishop Jean Pierre Augustine Mercellin Verot, the first bishop of Florida. Following his death in June 1876, mourners from all over the state began pouring into St. Augustine. To give the mourners time to arrive in the city, the funeral officials decided to place the bishop's body in a hermetically sealed iron coffin with a glass viewing window and then set the coffin inside a sawdust-lined pit. Mounds of ice were heaped inside the pit in an attempt to keep the body cool. On the day of the funeral, the blistering heat began interacting with the gases building up inside the sealed coffin. The mourners had no sooner lapsed into a respectful silence than the bishop's body exploded, shattering the viewing window and spewing flesh and putrid bodily fluids everywhere. After the coffin was resealed, it was taken to the funeral chapel, which was originally intended as the mausoleum for a Cuban priest named Father Felix Varela; he was buried in the crypts in 1855. According to the book *Weird Florida*, the slab covering the crypt was slid back, and Father Varela's bones were scooped up and placed in a pillowcase. After the bishop's remains were placed inside, the pillowcase was set next to it, and the slab was replaced.

The remains were undisturbed until 1911, when Father Varela's bones were returned to Cuba. On orders from Bishop Tanner of the Diocese of St. Augustine, the crypt was opened once again in 1975 to verify that the remains inside the coffin were actually those of Bishop Verot. As soon as the coffin's seal was broken, a horrible stench swept through the funeral chapel, forcing everyone inside to leave in a hurry. After the chapel aired out, the men returned to the coffin and took photographs of the bishop's remains. One of the photographs clearly showed the bishop's wooden teeth and the cross that was buried with him, proving that the remains were clearly those of Bishop Verot.

KEY WEST CEMETERY (KEY WEST)

Key West's first cemetery was a seaside cemetery close to Whitehead Point. On October 11, 1846, a disastrous hurricane washed most of the corpses out of their graves, depositing some of the of the bodies in the branches of the trees and others on top of sand dunes. In 1848, the cemetery was moved to the highest point in town—Solares Hill—which is only eighteen feet above sea level. Today, between 80,000 and 100,000 people lie inside Key West Cemetery. The nineteen-acre burial ground is the eternal resting place of a cross-section of Key West, including Cuban cigar makers, Bahamian mariners, Catholics, Protestants and Jews, Spanish-American War veterans, millionaires and paupers and people of all races.

Key West Cemetery is as unique as the city itself. In fact, some say it is the most unusual cemetery in the entire state. According to Charlie Carlson's book *Weird Florida*, some of the tombs, above and below ground, are stacked on top of each other. Space is at such a high premium in the cemetery that, in some cases, the remains and excess dirt were removed from the tombs and disposed of.

The colorful inscriptions on some of the tombstones have acquired a permanent place in the lore of Key West. The best-known inscription can be found on the tombstone of B.P. "Pearl" Roberts: "I Told You I Was Sick." The website Southernmost Ghosts includes other funny messages on tombstones in Key West Cemetery as well, such as "I Always Dreamed of Owning a Small Place in Key West," "If You Are Reading This, You Desperately Need a Hobby," and "Devoted Fan of Julio Iglesias."

A number of historical figures can also be found among the 100,000 graves in Key West Cemetery. "Sloppy Joe" Russell, owner of Sloppy Joe's Bar and friend of Ernest Hemingway, is buried here. So is General Abraham Lincoln Sawyer, a forty-inch-tall little person who died in 1939. The bronze statue of a sailor overlooks the graves of the 260 sailors who died when the battleship *Maine* exploded in Havana Harbor on February 15, 1898.

Not surprisingly, the "dear departed" spirits of some of the cemetery's occupants are still there. Some visitors to the tombs claim to have heard

The 260 sailors who were killed in the explosion of the battleship *Maine* on February 15, 1898, are buried at Key West Cemetery. *Wikimedia Commons*.

the voice of a little girl beckoning them to follow her to the grave of a twelve-year-old girl. Others have encountered the protective spirit of an angry Bahamian woman who appears to be searching for someone.

Author Lola Haskins related the strangest story connected with Key West Cemetery in her book *Fifteen Florida Cemeteries*. In 1927, Count Carl Von Cosel left his wife and daughters in Zephyrhills, Florida, and went to work as a radiologist in the naval hospital in Key West. His life changed forever in 1933 when a young Cuban woman named Elena Milagro de Hoyos showed up in his office for treatment for tuberculosis. He fell in love with the dark-haired, dark-eyed beauty from the moment he met her, despite the fact that both of them were already married to other people. She accepted the presents he brought her but insisted that she did not love him. He tried to cure her by administering electroshock treatments in his office and her home but to no avail. After just a few weeks, she was dead.

Von Cosel paid for her burial in the Key West Cemetery. He also purchased the plot next to hers for the purpose of building her final resting place: an elaborate mausoleum. When the mausoleum was completed three months later, Von Cosel exhumed Elena's coffin and transported it to the funeral parlor, where he cleaned up the body. He then transported her coffin to the new mausoleum. Night after night, people living in the neighboring houses saw Von Cosel enter Elena's mausoleum. It is said that he sat by her coffin, placed his hands on it and talked to her for hours at a time.

One night in April 1933, Von Cosel sneaked her body out of the mausoleum and placed it in a toy wagon, which he had brought to the cemetery. He took her body to a wingless airplane that he had stored behind the naval hospital and placed it inside. After immersing the body in fluids, he stuffed rags inside her corpse and doused it with perfume. He then moved her body to a shack he had purchased and placed Elena's body in an incubation tank. Following a hurricane in 1936, Von Cosel had to move Elena to a new house. By now, he was convinced that she could move around and talk to him. He soon became accustomed to sleeping with Elena's now-mummified corpse.

Von Cosel's weird relationship with the dead girl ended soon after hearing that someone had broken into Elena's mausoleum. When he got there, he found the sexton and Elena's sister, Nana, standing inside the open mausoleum. She asked Von Cosel to break the seal on her coffin so she could gaze into Elena's face one last time, but he refused. Two weeks later, Von Cosel relented and told Nana that she could visit her sister in his house. Understandably, Nana was horrified to find Elena's desiccated corpse lying in a bed. Nana dashed out of the house and contacted the sheriff, who removed the body four days later. Following a brief trial, Von Cosel was set free, and Elena was buried in an unmarked grave in Key West Cemetery. Von Cosel returned to Zephyrhills, where he devoted the rest of his life to writing his memoirs.

WORKS CITED

Books

Barnes, Jay. *Florida's Hurricane History*. Chapel Hill: University of North Carolina Press, 2007.

Berlitz, Charles. *The Bermuda Triangle*. New York: Avon Books, 1974.

Brown, Alan. *Ghosts of Florida's Gulf Coast*. Sarasota, FL: Pineapple Press, 2014.

Burrough, Bryan. *Public Enemies*. New York: Penguin, 2009.

Carlson, Charlie. *Weird Florida*. Ontario, Canada: Sterling Publishing Company, 2005.

Carmer, Carl. *Stars Fell on Alabama*. Tuscaloosa: University of Alabama Press, 1985.

Doyle, Stephanie Erickson. *Florida Unsolved Mysteries*. Springville, UT: Sweetwater Press, 2007.

Haskins, Lola. *Fifteen Florida Cemeteries*. Gainesville: University Press of Florida, 2011.

Lapham, Dave. *Ghosthunting Florida*. Cincinnati, OH: Clerisy Press, 2010.

Lewis, Chad, and Terry Fisk. *The Florida Road Guide to Haunted Locations*. Esau Claire, WI: Unexplained Research Company, 2010.

McAdie, Colin J., Christopher W. Landsea, Charles J. Neumann, Joan E. David and Eric S. Blake. *Tropical Cyclones of the North Atlantic Ocean, 1851–2006*. Asheville, NC: United States National Oceanic and Atmospheric Administration, 2009.

McCollum, John. *WPA Guide to Florida: The Federal Writers Project Guide to 1930s Florida, Written and Compiled by the Federal Writers' Project of the Works Progress Administration for the State of Florida.* New York: Pantheon, 1084.

Newton, Michael. *The Encyclopedia of Serial Killers.* New York: Checkmark Books, 2000.

Palsey, Fred. *Al Capone: The Biography of a Self-Made Man.* New York: Garden City Publishing, 1930.

Smith, Dusty. *Haunted Daytona Beach.* Charleston, SC: The History Press, 2007.

Winter, Robert. *Mean Men: The Sons of Ma Barker.* Netsource Distribution Services, 2000.

Websites

A&E. "How Danny Rolling, the 'Gainesville Ripper,' Was Caught." https://www.aetv.com.

ABC News. "Tropical Storm Nicole Sends Beachfront Homes into Ocean." https://abcnews.go.com.

———. "Woman Killed in Alligator Attack on Florida Golf Course: Sheriff." https://abcnews.go.com.

Admiral Cloudberg. "Lights in the Darkness: The Crash of Eastern Air Lines Flight 401." https://admiralcloudberg.medium.com.

American Society for Microbiology. "History of Yellow Fever in the U.S." asm.org.

AP News. "Residents Celebrate the Legendary—and Nasty—'Two-Toed Tom.'" https://apnews.com.

———. "The Story of Ted Bundy, 'The Very Definition of Heartless Evil.'" https://allthatsinteresting.com.

———. "The True Story of Danny Rolling, the Gainesville Ripper, Who Inspired 'Scream.'" https://allthatsinteresting.com.

———. "Why the FBI Thought Ma Barker Was America's Most Dangerous Mind in the 1930s." https://allthatsinteresting.com.

Arias, Pilar. "Update: Florida Woman Accused of Murder after Boyfriend Dies in Suitcase Faces Judge." Fox News, January 17, 2023. https://www.foxnews.com.

ASP Windows and Doors. "Top 10 Worst Hurricanes to Hit Florida." https://www.aspwindows.com.

ATI. "The Curious Case of Mary Reeser and Spontaneous Human Combustion." https://allthatsinteresting.com/.

Atlantic Oceanographic and Meteorological Laboratory. "Hurricane Andrew's Upgrade." https://www.aoml.noaa.gov.

Atlas Obscura. "Grave of Elizabeth Budd-Graham." https://www.atlasobscura.com.

———. "The Phillips Mausoleum." atlasobscura.com.

Barnes, Peter. "The Curious Case of Mary Reeser." Shutterbulky, https://www.shutterbulky.com.

Big Cat Rescue. "Florida Panther Facts." https://bigcatrescue.org.

Biography. "Aileen Wuornos. https://www.biography.com.

———. "Ma Barker." https://www.biography.com.

———. "Ted Bundy (1946–1989)." https://www.biography.com.

———. "Ted Bundy Killings: A Timeline of His Twisted Reign of Terror." https://www.biography.com.

Bowen, Jordan. "Three Shark Attacks Reported in Florida in Less Than a Week." Fox13 Tampa Bay, https://www.fox13news.com.

Boynton Beach Historical Society. "The Notorious Ashley Gang and Its Surprising Boynton Connections." www.boyntonhistory.org.

Bradford–Ma Barker House. "The Ma Barker Story." https://mabarkerhouse.org.

Breitenstein, Dave. "List: 24 Fatal Alligator Attacks in Florida Since 1973." https://www.news-press.com.

Britannica. "Ted Bundy." https://www.britannica.com

Capital Punishment in Context. "The Case of Aileen Wuornos—The Facts." https://capitalpunishmentincontext.org/cases/wuornos

CBS News. "CDC: 7 Deaths in Florida amid 'One of the Worst Outbreaks of Meningococcal Disease among Gay and Bisexual Men in U.S. History." https://www.cbsnews.com.

Center for Disease Control. "Florida's Fight: 1918 Flu Epidemic Wiped Out a State Poorly Equipped to Handle an Outbreak." cdc.gov.

City of Key West Florida. "Historic Key West City Cemetery." cityofkeywest-fl.gov.

Click Orlando. "15 Years Ago, the Groundhog Day Tornadoes Took 21 Lives in Florida." https://www.clickorlando.com.

———. "Ohio Woman Describes Shark Attack off Daytona Beach Shores." https://www.clickorlando.com.

———. "25 Years Since Deadly ValuJet 592 Crash, an Airline Mechanic Remains on the Run." https://www.clickorlando.com.

———. "226 Alligators Removed from Disney World Since Toddler's Death 5 Years Ago." https://www.clickorlando.com.

CNN. "Irma: A Hurricane for the History Books." https://www.cnn.com.

Copeland, Matthew. "A History of Shark Attacks in Florida." First Coast News, https://www.firstcoastnews.com.

Crime Investigation. "Ma Barker." https://www.crimeandinvestigation.co.uk.

Criminal Minds Wiki. "Aileen Wuornos." https://criminalminds.fandom.com.

———. "Danny Rolling." https://criminalminds.fandom.com.

Daytona Beach Blog. "Pinewood Cemetery." https://daytona-beach-blog.com.

DBpedia. "1909 Florida Keys Hurricane." https://dbpedia.org.

Eliza J. "The Babysitter from Hell." Medium, September 24, 2021. lightsonpod.medium.com.

FBI. "Barker/Karpis Gang." fbi.gov.

Florida Brace. "1998 Wildland Fire Outbreak." https://flbrace.org.

Florida Health. "It's a New Day in Public Health." https://www.floridahealth.gov/programs-and-services/public-health-campaigns/.

Florida Humanities. "Days of Trouble, Days of Hope." https://floridahumanities.org.

Florida Times-Union. "Alligator Attacks Are on Rise in Florida." www.jacksonville.com.

Fox35Orlando. "How Much Damage Did Hurricane Nicole Create in Florida? Estimate Already Above $500 Million." https://www.fox35orlando.com.

———. "How Strong Were Hurricane Nicole's Wind Gusts in Orlando and across Central Florida?" www.fox35orlando.com.

Free Press. "Graveyard Ghosts: Headless Spirit Roams the Pinewood Cemetery in Daytona Beach." tampafp.com.

Genzel, Joe. "Florida Accounted for Nearly 40 Percent of Shark Attacks Worldwide in 2021." Flipboard, https://flipboard.com.

Harrell, Scott. "The Curious Case of Mary Hardy Reeser." Spectrum News, October 20, 2020, https://www.baynews9.com.

———. "Haunted Guide to the Huguenot Cemetery in St. Augustine." https://www.ghostsandgravestones.com.

———. "The Haunted History of Captain Tony's Saloon in Key West." https://www.ghostsandgravestones.com.

Historic Tours of America. "Haunted Guide to St. Pauls Church Cemetery." https://www.ghostsandgravestones.com.

History.com. "Bermuda Triangle." www.history.com.

———. "Hurricane Donna Is Born." www.history.com.

Hoover, Erin. "Calvin C. Phillips Is the Unlikely Subject of Both Mystery and Legend." Tallahassee, September 1, 2018.

Hurricanes: Science and History. "1919 Florida Keys Hurricane." www.hurricanescience.org.

———. "1960—Hurricane Donna." www.hurricanescience.org.

———. "1965—Hurricane Betsy." www.hurricanescience.org.

I-4RouteGuide. "Interstate 4 Dead Zone—The Zone That Every American Fear!" i4routeguide.com.

Islamorada Times. "Keys History—The 1935 Labor Day Hurricane." https://www.islamoradatimes.com.

The Journalist's Resource. "Alligator Fatal Attacks and Encounters with Humans: Historical Data and Research." https://journalistsresource.org.

Kilgore, Jennifer. "Alligator Attacks in Florida." Enjuris, https://www.enjuris.com.

Library of Congress. "Rescue Train Swept off the Tracks by the 1935 Labor Day Hurricane." https://www.loc.gov.

Masters, Jeff. "Hurricane Nicole Hits Florida." Yale Climate Connections, https://yaleclimateconnections.org.

———. "Tropical Storm Nicole Intensifying as it Heads Toward the Bahamas and Florida." Yale Climate Connections, https://yaleclimateconnections.org.

Masters, Jeff, and Bob Henson. "Flooding, Heavy Rains to Sock the Bahamas and Florida This Week." Yale Climate Collections, https://yaleclimateconnections.org.

Maxwell, Colby. "Alligator Population by State." A–Z Animals, https://a-z-animals.com.

Merianos, Nick. "Labor Day Hurricane of 1935 Killed 408 People in the Florida Keys." Spectrum News, September 7, 2021. https://www.baynews9.com.

Miami Haunts. "Ghosts of Flight 401." https://miamihaunts.com.

Mob Museum. "Capone, Torrio and the Sunshine City, St. Petersburg, Florida." https://themobmuseum.org.

Murderpedia. "Bobby Joe Long." https://murderpedia.org.

———. "Christine Falling." https://murderpedia.org.

———. "David Alan Gore." https://murderpedia.org.

———. "Eddie Lee Moseley." https://murderpedia.org.

———. "Gerard John Schaefer." https://murderpedia.org.

———. "Oscar Ray Oline Jr." https://murderpedia.org.

Museum of Unnatural History. "The 'Mystery' of the Bermuda Triangle." www.unmuseum.org.

National Hurricane Center. "Hurricane Nicole Tropical Cyclone Update." https://www.nhc.noaa.gov.

National Library of Medicine. "Florida's Tuberculosis Epidemic. Public Health Response." https://pubmed.ncbi.nlm.nih.gov.

National Park Service. "Hurricane Andrew (1992)." https://www.nps.gov.

National Weather Service. "Hurricane Andrew's 30th Anniversary." https://weather.gov.

———. "Hurricane Irma 2017." https://weather.gov.

———. "The Hurricane of 1919." https://weather.gov.

New Haven Register. "Alligator Bites Off Arm of Swimming Florida Teen." https://www.nhregister.com.

News Channel 6. "Man Dies after Being Zipped into Suitcase, Girlfriend Arrested." https://www.wjbf.com.

News Channel 8. "Hurricane Irma: Record-Breaking Hurricane Impacted Florida 4 Years Ago." https://www.wfla.com.

News4Jax. "Flooding Saturates Coastal Areas of St. Augustine; Damaged Portion of A1A Reopens." https://www.news4jax.com.

News-Press. "Panther Attacks, Kills 500-Pound Pet Pony Named Maximus in Golden Gate Estates." www.news-press.com.

Newsweek. "Shark Attacks Woman During Florida Vacation." https://www.newsweek.com.

Nightly Spirits. "Myrtle Hill Cemetery in Tampa." https://nightlyspirits.com.

No. 1 Home Roofing. "The Worst Hurricanes in Florida's History." https://no1homeroofing.com.

Obringer, Lee Ann, and Patrick J. Kiger. "How the Bermuda Triangle Works." HowStuffWorks, adventure.howstuffworks.com.

Official Eastern Air Lines Flight 401-History, Photos, Survivors and Tribute. "The Crash of Eastern Airlines Flight 401." https://sites.google.com/site/eastern401/.

Oklahoma Historical Society. "Barker Gang." https://www.okhistory.org.

Old City Ghosts. "The Witch's Grave." https://oldcityghosts.com.

Old Town Manor. "Old Town Manor Legends of Captain Tony's Saloon." https://oldtownmanor.com.

Paranormal and Ghost Society. "Pinewood Historical Cemetery." www.paranoralghostsociety.org.

Partington, Verity. "The Ghosts of Eastern Flight 401." Medium, April 28, 2021. https://medium.com.

Planas, Antonio, and Marlene Lenthang. "Hurricane Nicole Unearths Suspected Native American Burial Site in Florida." www.nbcnews.com.

Reimann, Nicholas. "Covid Cases Spike in Florida as Bars and Restaurants Reopen at Full Capacity." Forbes, https://www.forbes.com.

Research Guides at Louisiana State University. "Hurricane Betsy." https://guides.lib.lsu.edu.

Salahieh, Nouran. "Nicole Becomes Post-Tropical Cyclone, Brings Rain to Northeast after Leaving a Trail of Destruction in Florida." CNN, https://www.cnn.com.

Salahieh, Nouran, Zoe Sottile and Renée Rigdon. "See Where Shark Attacks Are Happening across the US." https://www.cnn.com.

Skeptoid. "Grounding the Ghost of Flight 401." https://skeptoid.com.

Soapboxie. "Profile of a Serial Killer Cop: Gerard John Schaefer Jr." https://soapboxie.com.

Southernmost Ghosts. "Most Haunted Places in Key West." https://southernmostghosts.com.

Sprung, Shiomo. "Florida Ignored the Worst Tuberculosis Outbreak in 20 Years." Business Insider, July 9, 2012. https://www.businessinsider.com.

Starcasm. "True Crime: This Woman Put Her Boyfriend in a Suitcase and Left Him to Die." https://starcasm.net.

St. Pete Catalyst. "Vintage St. Pete: Capone, the Babe, the Gang's Jungle Prada." https://stpetecatalyst.com.

St. Paul's Key West. "Our History." https://stpaulskeywest.org.

Tampa Bay Times. "Capone House Still Haunts." https://www.tampabay.com.

TCPalm. "Ashley Gang: Notorious Outlaws Struck Fear in Stuart Residents." https://www.tcpalm.com.

———. "Firestorm of 1998: Wildfires Ravaged Florida 20 Years Ago, Burning Half a Million Acres." https://www.tcpalm.com.

10 Tampa Bay. "Gov. DeSantis Signs 4 Special Session Bills Aiming to Combat COVID-19 Vaccine Mandates." https://www.wtsp.com.

Thomas, Naomi. "CDC Investigates 'One of the Worst Outbreaks of Meningococcal Disease' in U.S. History among Gay and Bisexual Men in Florida." CNN, https://www.cnn.com.

TopTenz. "The I-4 Dead Zone: America's Most Haunted Highway." toptenz.net/the-4-dead-zone-americas-most-haunted-highway.php.

Travel Channel. "Castillo de San Marcos' History." https://www.travelchannel.com.

USA Today. "10-Year-Old Boy Gets Leg Amputated after Traumatic Shark Attack in Florida, Family Says." https://www.usatoday.com.

U.S. Geological Survey. "How Have Invasive Pythons Impacted Florida Ecosystems?" https://www.usgs.gov.

Vlamis, Kelsey. "Giant Invasive Pythons Run Rampant in Florida and Wreak Havoc on Native Species—but Python Hunters Are Here to Help." Business Insider, September 3, 2022. https://www.businessinsider.com.

Ward, Hannah. "3 Invasive Snakes in Florida." A–Z Animals, updated April 8, 2023. a-z-animals.com.

WCTV.tv. "Florida's Fight: 1918 Flu Epidemic Wiped Out a State Poorly Equipped to Handle an Outbreak." https://www.wctv.tv.

WebMD. "Meningococcal Disease Outbreak in Florida Epands: CDC." https://www.webmd.com.

———. "Yellow Fever." https://www.webmd.com.

WESH2. "On This Day: 21 Killed during Florida Tornado Outbreak on Groundhog Day." https://www.wesh.com.

West Palm Beach. "The Ashley Gang—West Palm Beach History." https://www.westpalmbeach.com.

Wink. "Dog Survives Florida Panther Attack, Loses Eye in Golden Gate Estates." https://www.winknews.com.

———. "Victims of '96 ValuJet Plane Crash in Everglades Remembered." https://www.winknews.com.

World Health Organization. "Coronavirus Disease (COVID-19)." https://www.who.int.

World Vision. "2017 Hurricane Irma: Facts, FAQs, and How to Help." https://www.worldvision.org.

WPBF. "250 Alligators Removed from Walt Disney World in Last 5 Years." https://www.wpbf.com.

WPTV. "Florida Health Urges Public Keep 'Closer Eye' as Deadly Meningitis Outbreak Worsens." https://www.wptv.com.

WUSF. "Gov. DeSantis Announces Phase 3 Reopening, Lifts Restrictions on Restaurants." wusfnews.wusf.usf.edu/politics-issues/2020-09-25/desantis-announces-phase-3-reopening-lifts-restrictions-on-restaurants

Journals and Magazines

Barker, Eirlys. "A Sneaky, Cowardly Enemy: Tampa's Yellow Fever Epidemic of 1887–88." *Scholar Commons* 8, no. 2 (1986): 4–22.

Cangiolosi, John P., Andrew S. Latto and Robbie Berg. "Hurricane Irma (AL112017)." *National Hurricane Center Tropical Cyclone Report*, August–September 2017.

Delaney, Bill. "Yellow Jax: The 1888 Jacksonville Yellow Fever Epidemic." *Jaxson Magazine*, August 2021.

Dunn, Gordon E. "The Hurricane Season of 1960." *Monthly Weather Review*, September 2013.

Fairlie, Margaret C. "The Yellow Fever Epeidemic of 1888 in Jacksonville." *Florida Historical Quarterly* 19, no. 2 (1940): 95–108.

Frazier, Ian. "The Snakes That Ate Florida." *Smithsonian Magazine*, July 2019.

Hendrickson, V.L. "Al Capone's Miami Beach Mansion, Saved from Demolition, Sells for $15.5 Million." *Mansion Global*, October 2021.

Hoover, Erin. "Calvin C. Phllips Is the Unlikely Subject of Both Mystery and Legend." *Tallahassee Magazine*, September 2018.

Melssen, Maria. "The Great White Plague: Tuberculosis in Key West, 1917–1945." *Tequesta* 71 (2011): 59–76. dpanther.fiu.edu.

Michaels, Will. "A New Look at Al Capone in St. Pete—Part 1." *Northeast Journal*, July 2015.

———. "A New Look at Al Capone in St. Pete—Part 2." *Northeast Journal*, September 2015.

Reimann, Nicholas. "Covid Cases Spike in Florida As Bars and Restaurants Reopen at Full Capacity." *Forbes*, September 2020.

Suggs, Arnold L. "The Hurricane Season of 1965." *Monthly Weather Review* 94, no. 3 (1966): 183–91.

Tisdale, C.F. "The Weather and Circulation of September 1960." *Monthly Weather Review*, September–December 1960.

Newspapers

Balona, Patricio G. "Shark Bites Daytona Man; Third Incident Reported in New Smyrna Beach This Year." *Daytona Beach News Journal*, July 3, 2022.

Bella, Timothy. "Florida Teen's Leg to Be Amputated after Weekend of Shark Attacks." *Washington Post*, July 4, 2022.

Blowing Very Hard along the Southern Coast." *Altoona Tribune*, October 19, 1910.

Charles, Jackqueline. "Nicole Brings 'Extensive Flooding' to Bahamas as It Intensifies to a Hurricane." *Miami Herald*, November 16, 2022.

Chung, Christine. "Two Alligators Fatally Attack Florida Woman after She Falls into Pond." *New York Times*, July 21, 2022.

Conti, Allie. "Hunter Says He Was Attacked in First-Ever Florida Panther Attack." *Broward Palm Beach New Times*, April 20, 2014.

Esto Herald. "Festival Honors a Legendary Gator." August 30, 1987.

Etters, Karl. "Skull Stolen More Than a Decade Ago Still Missing." *Tallahassee Democrat*, October 31, 2014.

Fears, Darryl. "Disney Knew Its Property Had Alligators. It Caught Hundreds before a Boy Was Killed." *Washington Post*, November 3, 2017.

Fiallo, Josh, Kirby Wilson, Ana Ceballo and Doug Hanks. "Florida's Bars to Reopen with 50 Percent Capacity on Monday." *Tampa Bay Times*, September 10, 2020.

Fitchburg Sentinel. "75-Mile Winds Said Sweeping Key West Area." October 5, 1948.

Holland, Mayor Milissa. "20 Years Later: Palm Coast Remembers the 1998 Fires." *Palm Coast Observer*, June 5, 1998.

Jacob, Mary Kay. "Al Capone's Miami Beach Mansion Saved from Demolition Sells for $15.5M." *New York Post*, October 8, 2021.

Jones, Judson, Jasper Williams-Ward and Johnny Diaz. "Tropical Storm Nicole Forecast to Become Hurricane as It Nears Florida." *New York Times*, November 8, 2022.

Maxwell, Scott. "Wrestling with Absurdity: DeSantis Shuts Down Most Businesses, but Gives WWE a Pass." *Orlando Sentinel*, April 19, 2020.

Mertens, Richard. "Florida Brought Back Its Panthers. Can People Live with Them?" *Christian Science Monitor*, July 22, 2021.

Miami New Times. "Irmageddon: Thousands of Miamians Just Had Their First Taste of Hurricane Misery." September 13, 2017.

Mower, Lawrence. "Gov. Ron DeSantis Won't Shut Down Florida. Here's Who He's Talking to About That." *Tampa Bay Times*, March 25, 2020.

Mower, Lawrence, and Allison Ross. "DeSantis Invalidates COVID Rules Statewide: No Need to Police People at this Point." *Tallahassee Democrat*, January 1, 2022.

New York Times. "Havoc by Storm in Key West." October 12, 1909.

———. "Hurricane Nears the Florida Coast." October 5, 1910.

Persaud, Chris. "Coronavirus Florida: Patients in Florida Had Symptoms as Early as January." *Florida Times Union*, May 5, 2020.

The Scotsman. "West Indian Hurricane." October 18, 1910.

Spokane Daily Chronicle. "Hurricane in Cuba Coasts Many Lives." October 17, 1918.

St. Lucie County Tribune. "Key West Was Half Ruined." October 15, 1909.

Sumner, H.C. "North Atlantic Hurricanes and Tropical Disturbances of 1948." *Monthly Weather Review*, December 1948.

Traub, Alex. "Alligator Kills Florida Man Retrieving Frisbees in Lake, Officials Say." *New York Times*, May 31, 2022.

Washington Post. "West Indian Hurricane." October 19, 1910.

ABOUT THE AUTHOR

Alan Brown teaches English at the University of West Alabama in Livingston, Alabama. Alan has written primarily about southern ghost lore, a passion that has taken him to haunted places throughout the entire Deep South, as well as parts of the Midwest and the Southwest. Alan's wife, Marilyn, accompanies him on these trips and occasionally serves as his "ghost magnet." Her encounters with the spirit world have been incorporated in a number of Alan's books.